HIGH INFATUATION

HIGH INFATUATION

*A Climber's Guide to
Love and Gravity*

STEPH DAVIS

THE MOUNTAINEERS BOOKS

THE MOUNTAINEERS BOOKS
*is the nonprofit publishing arm of The Mountaineers, an organization
founded in 1906 and dedicated to the exploration, preservation, and
enjoyment of outdoor and wilderness areas.*

1001 SW Klickitat Way, Suite 201, Seattle, WA 98134

© 2007 by Steph Davis

First edition: first printing 2007, second printing 2012

Manufactured in the United States of America

Copy Editor: Julie Van Pelt
Cover Design: Karen Schober
Book Design and Layout: Mayumi Thompson

Cover photograph: *Steph and Fletch at home in their truck at Indian Creek, Utah* (photo by
Eric Perlman)
Back cover photograph: *Freeing El Cap in a day* (photo by Heinz Zak)
Frontispiece: *Steph Davis freeing the Salathe Wall, El Cap* (photo by Jimmy Chin)

Library of Congress Cataloging-in-Publication Data
Davis, Steph, 1972-
  High infatuation : a climber's guide to love and gravity / by Steph Davis.
     p. cm.
  ISBN 1-59485-065-8 (paperbound)
  1. Mountaineering—Guidebooks. 2. Mountaineers—United States—Biography.
  3. Women mountaineers—United States—Biography. I. Title.
GV200.D38 2007
796.52'2—dc22
                              2006036711

TO FLETCH

Lovers don't finally meet somewhere.
They're in each other all along.
—Rumi

CONTENTS

1

HIGH INFATUATION

Gamble everything for love,
if you're a true human being.
—Rumi

I STARTED CLIMBING ON GROUNDHOG DAY 1991, at a tiny little cliff near the Potomac River in Maryland. Of course, I wasn't out there for some kind of holiday celebration, but many years later I had a sudden vivid memory of sitting in dappled sun, exclaiming "I can't believe it's Groundhog Day and it's warm enough to be in a tee shirt!"

At every moment, single decisions affect life's direction, but it is rare when they are so easily identifiable as the day I decided to skip my freshman calculus class at the University of Maryland and try this mysterious thing called rock climbing.

I had been a nonathlete all my life. I'd been put in front of a piano since the age of three, and I spent my time practicing piano or flute, reading, and doing homework. Yes, nerdy. As a kid I did like poking around in the woods, but certainly not in any specific or sports-oriented way. But oddly, in my last year of high school, I suddenly became interested in mountain biking and started enthusiastically tearing through the woods and then around the University of Maryland campus on my bike. I loved it to pieces, literally, and spent many happy hours taking my bike apart and putting it back together again. This was before the advent of shock suspension, and before helmets became common, and I managed to crash and knock myself out many times, most embarrassingly while cutting across a hilly lawn between classes.

OPPOSITE: The Salathe Headwall, El Cap (photo by Jimmy Chin)

This newfound passion was what turned me into a rock climber. I was sitting outside the cafeteria one sunny day, eating lunch with my bike propped beside me. The university was not a particularly outdoorsy place. Most people walked around in dress shoes and were usually found indoors. Although my scruffy clothes and hand-painted bike would not have caused a second glance in Boulder, in College Park I stuck out like a sore thumb. I think I must have been the least worldly eighteen-year-old around. Despite filling my brain with thousands of books over the years, I was not very clued in to the complex rings of social hierarchies that circled my own life. In a pattern that would take me years to notice, a fit, attractive guy from Wyoming stopped his own bike next to me and engaged me in a conversation, eventually suggesting that we go rock climbing together. Although I had no idea what rock climbing might be, I got the feeling that it could have some things in common with mountain biking, and without questioning why anyone would want to do it with someone who had never even heard of it, I immediately agreed to go.

You might wonder how a person who did almost nothing but read books had managed to never hear of climbing, not even mountaineering. I have no idea. All I can say is that I grew up in the suburbs, outdoor sports had not yet boomed into the mainstream, and I read mostly classics. Through my entire childhood, my favorite book was *Brave New World,* which was lying around the house, a relic from one of my mom's college courses. On any boring day, I ended up rereading it, to the point of knowing most of it by heart. By the time I realized it was more than a sci-fi story, I had irreversibly absorbed all the social criticism. This may have dramatically influenced my outlook on life and turned me into a subversive at a very young age. Something did, so I may as well blame it on Huxley. At any rate, then, as now, I lived in my own little world, and climbing had never appeared on the radar.

On that very first day of climbing, slipping and flailing my way up a thirty-foot rock slab, I was infatuated. I immediately restructured my entire life to direct everything toward climbing. Little did I know that I was experiencing the safest, least dramatic type of climbing imaginable, with a toprope above me on the tiny cliff that kept me from falling more than six inches. To me, it was like a door had been opened to another world.

Over the subsequent fifteen years, my infatuation with climbing has not dimmed, although it has matured into an enduring love. I have learned the joys and limitations of the many disciplines that make up climbing, from the intensity of short boulder problems, to the complexity of aid climbing on ropes and gear while living on big walls, to moving fast, alpine style, over snow and ice in the mountains, to pushing the edge of my limits on free climbing projects, and perhaps the purest of all, the flawless movement of free solo climbing without ropes or protection, when the mind truly empties, stripped to nothing but the rock.

My pursuit of climbing was initiated by impulse. In reality it was never a choice, but rather a surrender to the inevitable. Even now, supposedly older and wiser, I make my most fundamental life decisions impetuously, based on what feels right inside, and I never look back. It's the only thing I can do.

Although I reshuffled my life to accommodate my newfound passion for climbing, I did finish college, and even got a master's degree. I took advantage of U of M's student exchange program and spent my sophomore year at Colorado State University. I later returned to CSU for grad school and of course used mountaineering literature for my required thesis. At the time, the literature department did not consider this a valid field of study, but thanks to my open-minded and supportive thesis committee, I was allowed to do it. I'm sure these wise professors realized that anything else I might have chosen would be a lifeless, superficial disaster and would have bored us all to tears. And in fact, I was so enthusiastic that I finished my thesis a year ahead of schedule, which is a little embarrassing even for a graduate student.

The happy coexistence of academics and climbing came to a grinding halt when I finished my degree. I moved to Estes Park, Colorado, with my boyfriend Dean, to be close to the Longs Peak Diamond and earn money by waitressing for the summer. I thought I wanted to go to the University of Utah, in Salt Lake, and continue in a PhD program in the fall. My professors in Colorado had encouraged me to enter the American studies program, thinking it would accommodate my somewhat eclectic interests in mountaineering, natural science,

Summit of Poincenot, Patagonia (photo by Dean Potter)

social history, and literature. However, when I visited the university I was aghast at the emphasis on theory. I was one of those literature students who wanted to read books and history, and draw ideas about the world from them. The new trend was literary theory, which all the hip intellectuals were studying. They didn't even seem to read normal books. Instead, they read the books and articles that the theorists wrote, then theorized about the theorists' theories. It all seemed pretentious and pointless to me, and not even about literature. At CSU, some of the older, down-to-earth professors felt the same way, and I had been spared most of it except for a few token theory classes and having to invent some line about how my blatantly nontheory-based thesis actually had some grounding in literary theory, in case anyone asked. At

U of Utah, they definitely asked. In fact, everyone I met in the English department seemed to be obsessed with theory. Out of habit, I tried to give the right answers and get out of there, but when I received the acceptance to the PhD program in the mail, along with a teaching assistantship offer, I threw it away.

I wavered just once, at the end of the summer in Estes. Being a waitress in a burrito joint was not very pleasant. Dean and I were both helplessly controlled by the warring pulls of our strong passions for each other and climbing, and this made life chaotic and dramatic. My parents hated everything I was doing and predicted that my future would involve welfare, misery, and penury. At the last possible moment, I enrolled in law school in Boulder, fearing that my LSATs would expire before I could use them and thinking I might as well give it a try. It only took a week to realize that it felt wrong. The idyll was over. I could no longer continue the tranquil, respectable lifestyle of attending university. I had no choice. I had to become a dirtbag climber.

For the next seven years, I lived first in my grandmother's hand-me-down Oldsmobile sedan, with all the passenger seats removed, and then, luxuriously, in a used Ford Ranger. Sometimes I worked as a waitress, other times as a climbing guide, while Dean and I regularly entered and exited each other's lives. I devoted myself completely to rock climbing and, as my horizons expanded, to mountain adventures. Along the way, I fell in love with Moab, Utah, and made it my home by acquiring a storage unit and a library card there. In Moab, I fell in love with a little mixed-breed heeler dog named Fletcher, and she managed to fit right in with my vagabond ways.

I constantly worried that my life was a wreck and careening toward destitution. But as the years went by, I became less nervous. Living in a truck requires a very low overhead, and although I was outrageously poor, it was no different from being a student except that I had to pay for health insurance. I was able to afford food, thrift store clothing, and the occasional book if there was no library at hand. The rest of my money went for trips to Patagonia and Asia, assisted by small grants from climbing organizations. I realized that angst over the future was pointless.

The fact is that I am completely incapable of doing anything I am not passionate about, except as a short-term necessity (waitressing, for example). Ironically, the path has so far led me to an existence in which, at the moment, I am more content than I could have predicted. I still have a Ford Ranger and am prone to living in it. Dean and I married, but then split for good after seven years, and Fletch passed away from old age in 2009. My first and most beloved sponsors have given way to new ones, and I am now blissfully married to a French-Canadian base jumper named Mario. We live in Moab with another small dog who was abandoned on the res and a little black cat who moved in one day. Life keeps changing and evolving, but in some ways stays the same.

Throughout those fast-paced years, I kept countless journals and wrote articles and short prose poems when the spirit moved me. Usually after a big climbing trip, or a really significant experience, I feel compelled to write. Some of these pieces were published by various climbing publications, others have been written for myself, and a final few were written for this book. Together they make up a small history of living the climbing life.

2

SAFE PLACES

Freedom from fear comes only to those who lead a pure life.
The yogi knows that he is different from his body,
which is a temporary house for his spirit.
To the yogi death is the sauce that adds zest to life.
When he has linked his entire being to the lord,
what then shall he fear?

—B. K. S. Iyengar

GROWING UP NEAR WASHINGTON, D.C., I was well aware of the city's murder statistics. In my freshman year of college at University of Maryland, women were officially warned not to walk outside at night alone. I learned not to make eye contact with strangers on the street, and to avoid talking to people I didn't know. These antisocial habits aren't always appreciated in the West, where I now live. But fear dies hard.

When I first went climbing, I felt blissfully safe away from people. I think that freedom from fear was part of what pulled me in. I like to be alone, a lot more than most people I know. I like to run alone, climb alone, hang out alone. I spent my twenties traveling and living in the back of a truck, mostly accompanied only by a forty-pound dog. It's actually a miracle I've survived this long. I have probably severely depleted my luck account.

Climbing drove me away from Maryland to Fort Collins, Colorado. Between classes at Colorado State University, I would ride my mountain bike to Horsetooth Reservoir and spend hours alone at the boulders, trying to decipher the old, extremely difficult John Gill

OPPOSITE: At Rio Blanco base camp, Patagonia (photo by Steph Davis)

boulder problems that he had marked with tiny white arrows, back in the sixties before bouldering was even considered a sport. I am still amazed by how far ahead of his time Gill was as a climber. His most difficult, test-piece climbs on these boulders remain test pieces nearly fifty years later, despite advances in climbing. I loved the quiet afternoons at Horsetooth, looking at the reservoir, feeling the grainy sandstone, imagining moments in time when other climbers were in this same place, touching these same rocks.

In the three years I lived in Fort Collins, I went to the well-known climbing destinations of Eldorado and Boulder Canyons only about four times. I instinctively shied away from the crowded, urban feel of Boulder. Instead, I became passionate about Wyoming. With friends from Fort Collins, I made many visits to Fremont Canyon, a beautiful, isolated climbing area. I learned how to lead climb at Devils Tower, a peaceful basalt monolith that rises out of the plains. I felt comfortable in the wide-open spaces of Wyoming, a place where life seemed uncomplicated and pure. And the first time I drove into the serene red canyons of Moab, Utah, I knew I was home.

For years I foolishly believed that staying away from cities and highways would keep me safe from harm. The sad truth is that any remote place that's too easy to reach isn't safe for a woman. For me, the thought of getting hit by icefall or falling from a rock face are totally acceptable possibilities. The idea of being hurt by a person is not. It always surprises me to hear people talk about climbing being dangerous. I have always felt safest alone on the side of a hard-to-reach wall or a mountain. Although I understand that I could die in the mountains, I trust the hand of nature, and I know it will do me no harm.

People seem to change and do confusing things. Places, on the other hand, I can count on.

FALLING

I'm tired from the drive to Wyoming. The headlights flick over sage-brush and flash the deer rimming the road. I try to see the landscape that I remember as beautiful, but the moon is too new, and I've only been here once before. My climbing partner and I jump a little as the car bumps onto the bridge over the canyon. It's a wild-looking bridge, made to fit this strangely narrow canyon, only about a hundred feet wide and a hundred feet deep. I remember how the water is pinched between the walls, dammed and sluggish, barely covering the shadowy boulders on the bottom.

Climbing the canyon walls can be intimidating. Once we slide down our ropes to a ledge above the water, up the rock is the only way out. The devious nature of the pink granite keeps most climbers away, leaving Fremont Canyon oddly isolated. Often the only sound I hear as I climb up the walls is my own tight breathing and the echoed plops of stones that Mike tosses into the still water.

The ribbed surface of the bridge vibrates the car and jiggles us into speech. "Do you know about those two girls who got thrown off the bridge?" Mike asks. The car gives a final bump off the metal and onto the dirt road. I spin around, groping for a view past the scaffolded sides of the small bridge, but the darkness makes it appear to float in the air.

"What? What are you talking about? Someone threw people off that? My God, you'd die for sure. That's horrible. Did they die?"

"One did," he says. Behind us the bridge spirals away into the darkness.

For the next week, the girls are all I can think about. Lowering down ropes to start our climbs, I glance furtively at the water, trying to calculate depth. I look at the varying greens of boulders underneath and estimate their distance below the water's surface. When I fall climbing, ten, twenty feet before the rope catches me, I try to imagine what it would be like to keep going. Mike gets tired of repeating the vague details he knows from hearsay and starts to look uncomfortable with the subject. All week, the canyon stays deserted; the stillness of this place feels laced with something.

At noon one day, the heat makes it impossible to climb. We search for shade, but sagebrush seems to be the tallest vegetation here. All the rest is cacti and granite, sand and gravel. We sit by the car on the rim of the canyon, sweating and looking at the bridge. The green water between the canyon walls starts to look inviting.

"Let's rappel off the bridge into the water," I say.

Mike instantly snaps out of his wilted celery impression and starts grabbing ropes and slings from the trunk.

"Okay, but let's hang the ropes short so we can slide off the ends into the water."

"How short?" I ask.

"How about twenty feet? There aren't any rocks right under the middle of the bridge."

We carry the gear to the bridge, tying knots and looping slings around the wide metal supports. Looking straight down I can't get any depth perception, so I lower the ropes until I see the ends touch water and then pull several arm lengths back up before tying them off. Now the two ropes are hanging straight down from the bridge, ends dangling far below.

The beginning is the awkward part. Attached to the rope with my harness, I have to clamber over and through the guard scaffold to get free of the bridge. Halfway over the edge, I get pinched between the rope and the side of the bridge. I hold the rope tight, shove hard, and spring free of the metal.

Suddenly I'm dangling like a spider, my eyes level with the bottom of the bridge. The round rivet caps on the beams are as big and smooth as tea saucers. I rub one with my free hand, and then Mike is beside me on his rope. We look at each other like kids at an amusement park and laugh gleefully.

Slowly, to savor the novelty, I slide down the rope. When I use this rappeling technique in climbing, there's almost always a rock wall in front of me. And rappeling is not something climbers do for fun; it's a procedure that requires very little skill and that I usually associate with retreat—an accident, failure, or bad weather. In the back of my mind always lurks the fear that the rope could get cut or that I'll make a mistake and somehow slip off the end. Some of the best climbers in the world have died this way, taken in by darkness, fatigue, clouded judgment. But now, on a hot July day, this rap is different. We are doing it on purpose, for fun, and we intend to rappel off the ends of the ropes. I've never done that before, and I wonder if my instinct for self-preservation will let me do it.

Halfway down the rope, I can see a beautiful crack across from me running up the wall under the far end of the bridge. I stop to look more carefully—it looks like something I'll want to climb later. As I negotiate with the slowly turning rope, trying to stop spinning, I suddenly realize what a strange place I'm in. I'm almost exactly halfway in the middle of this canyon, three dimensionally. I am a point in the center of a cube formed by the water, bridge, and canyon walls, and I can stay here in space for as long as I want. And suddenly the story of the two girls comes rushing into my mind, because they were in this spot once too, but only for a fraction of a second. It happened when I was a child, two thousand miles away, but I've thought it over so often since hearing about it that I feel like I saw it.

I look up to where the rope presses against the bridge and the July sun wipes away into star-pricked winter night. I can see them, the two sisters, drawn with terror, struggling against the stranger. They realized a few miles out of Casper that this hitch was going the wrong way, out to Fremont Canyon. It's cold, and their clothes are torn, but after he forces his way into them, the pain and tears burn hot. And then I see, at the very brink of the bridge, there's no point in struggling more. Something bigger is pulling. It's almost a relief to feel his hands peel off—no more pain and terror, just the fall. It's almost inviting, so soft and dark. Numbed, I slip out of the air and the water surface batters cruelly before I break through it.

Gasping, we pop up and swim the few yards to the gravelly shore. The ropes dangle merrily behind us. My harness is soaking wet, and my legs sting from slapping the water surface, but I'm cool and awake now. We scramble up the narrow tongue of loose rocks and dirt, back to the road. It's the same slope she crawled out on ten years ago, with her hip shattered and her sister dead, to lie on the bridge and wait for the end of an empty Wyoming night.

Falling climbers beside the sisters, Fremont Canyon bridge, Wyoming (Steph Davis collection)

At the end of the week, I watch the bridge disappear around a curve in my rearview mirror, still thinking about the sisters. As always, my mind is wrapped in questions. Why did he do it? How could he do it? Whatever happened to the girl who lived?

Two Julys later, I'm back in Fremont. I have a new climbing partner and I want to climb harder routes. Miraculously, the port-a-potty has even been emptied. And this time I am the one telling the story of the two sisters as the car jitters over the bridge. "What?" Joe says. "Someone threw people off here? What happened to them?"

My mind rushes back to the cold black falling, terror, pain. "One died," I say. "It's pretty hot. Do you feel like rapping off the bridge? We can leave the ends short and fall into the water."

This time I take the ends up about forty feet before fixing the ropes to the bridge, and the slap of the water feels like a leather strap when it hits me. As I step out of the water I see a white drawing on the rock wall to my left, the wall that runs up to the end of the bridge.

"Will you look at this," I say aloud in disgust. "Why do people always have to deface the rock?"

I walk over to look more closely. The outline is rather beautiful in the way that graffiti often is. The even white line stands out starkly against the dark pink granite, curving out two female figures. Their hands are joined, their other limbs relaxed, and the pink stone outlined between their hips and locked hands makes a heart shape. The way their hair floats up above them makes them look like they're falling as gently as fairies in a storybook. As from a great distance, I hear the water dropping off Joe's body when he emerges on the shore behind me. To the right of the white sisters, words are painted carefully on the wall.

Two souls
lost to us
victims of violence
tears wept for
lost innocence
beauty and
love.
May flights of angels
escort them
to their peace.
Pray to God
that no more follow.
—M. Carr, 1992

There they are, falling again, perennially, frozen in middrop without a rope. They are held beautifully, with streaming hair and delicate limbs, inscribed in white on the pink rock. No blood, no terror.

After a long time, we scramble back up to the bridge. The first car I've yet seen at Fremont rumbles over and slows beside us. Wet and smelly from the fermenting stagnant water, we still receive a neighborly greeting from the pickup driver. He's barrel-chested and Wyoming friendly, a local climber who's thrilled to see strangers taking an interest in his home crag.

"Do you know anything about that painting down there?" I ask immediately, even before exchanging the typical climbers' talk about routes.

"Well, yes," he replies. "That painting just showed up a couple weeks ago. You know about the two sisters that got kidnapped and raped ten years ago? Well, they also got pushed off the bridge here. One died, and one crawled out with a broken hip. She crawled down the road and a couple found her half-dead in the early morning—took her to the hospital. She testified against the two men and they're in the Wyoming State Prison now. They'll never get out. Names are Kennedy and Jenkins."

He pauses to rub his short sandy mustache. I get the feeling that this is a long speech for him, and that he's recited it before. I look at Joe and tug at the leg loop of my wet harness. I didn't know there were two men who'd taken the sisters. It makes sense. I'd always sort of wondered how just one man could rape two girls and keep one or the other from running off during the whole thing.

"So someone just decided to paint a picture about it?" I ask.

"Well, now, this is the strange part."

I feel the sun burning the thick green water off my shoulders. My tangled hair hangs down, stinking and heavy, and I think of the rippling white manes of the sisters reaching up, a hundred feet under the spot where I am standing.

"The sister who lived made a new life for herself out in Casper. She recovered and became a deejay on the radio. She was a big success story. But ten years later, last month, that is, she drove out here with her boyfriend. They'd been drinking a little and she went over to look off the bridge, and when her boyfriend came back she was gone. Jumped off. My wife Carrie says it looks inviting at night, she says it's all soft and dark. Well, you know it's pretty shallow and rocky down there. She died that time. Just jumped off in the dark."

Three times, then. And the third jump is suspended on the wall below. I look back at him, stunned, at his pleasant face framed in the open pickup window. At my back, the bridge side corrals us in like calves around a rancher's truck. Down below the water sits, glowing dull green in the hot sun. Carrie says at night it looks inviting, soft and dark. Even now I can feel it. The closer I get to the edge, the more I can feel the fall. It's not good for a climber to think about falling this much. The water has dried on my skin, leaving my face tight. The two men are starting to look at me—am I imagining it, or are they studying me more closely?

"That's quite a story," I say, moving away from the bridge scaffold, in closer to the solid bright truck. I can feel the sisters white beneath me, falling.

THE ROCK AND I

I used to think it was all about pull-ups, and I did a lot of them.

I sit below the crack. Red desert. Sandstone stretches endlessly around me.

I put a flower barrette in my hair, like an offering, and stand at the base. Ropeless, I feel naked yet free, as pure as the crack. I haven't done a pull-up in months.

The crack runs above me, magical in its simplicity. I think of the chains of DNA twining inside my body and I ponder the mystery of this crack. I need to move into it, find the cadence and match it.

I breathe deeply. I am working for the low, even beat that comes at the height of a mountain run. I fix my eyes, hands, and feet into the stone and let my breaths lead me up. The crack clasps my hands and shoes as gently and firmly as a lover. I can almost feel my double helixes untwisting and straightening to meet it.

Everything becomes a perfect line; we move all together. Fear is an unknown concept. I am not alone here. I am not even me. I am one more strand, weaving into the rhythm.

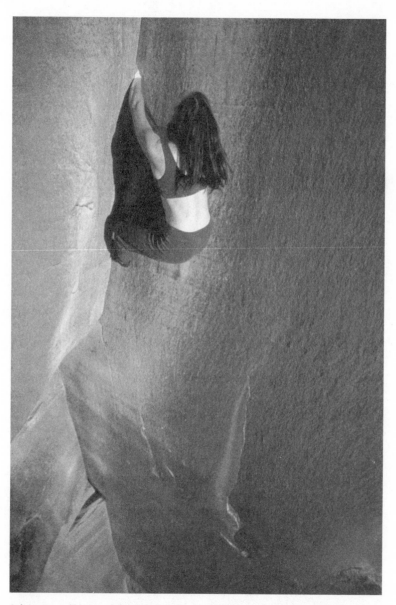

Soloing Incredible Hand Crack, Indian Creek, Utah (photo by Kennan Harvey)

3

BIENVENIDOS A PATAGONIA

The mind is impetuous and stubborn, strong and willful,
as difficult to harness as the wind.
—The Bhagavad Gita

AFTER MY SHORT-LIVED CAREER as a law student in Boulder, I finally surrendered to the gypsy call that all devoted climbers feel. I hightailed it to Rifle, Colorado, and spent blissful days in the idyllic, flower-filled canyon until the temperatures turned cold. Soon I found myself in Yosemite, and then Hueco Tanks, Texas, ricocheting against Dean like a pinball. It was impossible for us to avoid each other. We loved all the best climbing areas in America and were helplessly drawn there in the high seasons.

As winter ended, I was almost out of money and knew it was time to settle down, at least long enough to earn some cash. Moab was undoubtedly the place for me, and I started waiting tables at a high-volume tourist haven, Eddie McStiff's. Dean followed me to Moab, and we agreed to try again. We couldn't expect to hold down jobs while living in our cars, so for four hundred dollars I bought an ancient, tiny travel trailer from the guy who owned the local climbing shop. My best friend Lisa embarked on her decade-plus career as second mother to me and graciously invited me to park it in her dirt driveway. I was thrilled! My own home! Sharing it with a six-and-a-half-foot giant was a little tight, but still far more spacious than a tent.

We did fine until the summer heat arrived, and the trailer became an oven. Dean was also waiting tables, at the Fat City Smokehouse, and

OPPOSITE: Primrose Dihedrals, Moses, Utah (photo by Charlie Fowler)

our tempers were frayed beyond repair. By the end of the summer, we had broken up again, and thinking about my life just scared me. Still, as unenthusiastic as I was about my so-called career, the money was good, and I was obsessing on the hard cracks at Indian Creek. Even in the roasting hundred-degree-plus summer, I would somehow scrounge up a partner and be at a shady cliff by 6:00 AM, able to get in four hours of climbing before the sun hit the rock. This schedule fit perfectly with my night shifts at Eddie's, except for the small detail of sleep.

At Indian Creek, I met a guy from Colorado named Charlie. He was as passionate about the desert cracks as I was, and we began climbing together regularly. As winter approached, Charlie started talking about Patagonia. Everything he said made it sound like the Longs Peak Diamond, but better. The pictures were stunning. White, white granite spires against a crystal blue sky, rimmed by pure, snowy glaciers. Charlie described the cleanest granite crack climbing imaginable. He seemed unconcerned that I'd never put on mountain boots before and didn't know how to jumar up a rope or pound in a pin. Though I lacked some basic aid climbing and alpine skills, I was a disproportionately strong rock climber and a fast learner, and I was almost frighteningly driven. Eddie McStiff's closed for the winter and put the waitresses on unemployment . . . my unemployment checks would almost exactly cover the cost of a plane ticket to Patagonia!

MAYBE THE SWISS WERE RIGHT

After a month of rain, wind, snow, sleet, and numerous other forms of precipitation I never knew existed, I was growing skeptical of Charlie's insistence that good weather really did exist in Patagonia. Climbing is believing, and to date, I'd stood on only one summit and descended in a storm.

"Are you going to come back?" I asked another first-timer as he packed his soggy tent.

"I'm sure the routes are great here, but it doesn't do you much good if the weather's always too bad to climb them," he said dejectedly.

Over the next month of continuous storms, I learned the names and behaviors of eight different kinds of clouds. I listened to tales of the now legendary (at least in the base camp) Ten Splitter Days of early December, which Charlie and I arrived just in time to miss. And I began to take a desperate interest in the weather theories that were swirling around Campo Bridwell.

Charlie had been sticking to the calendar method all along. He claimed that late January had to show better weather—because it always did—and he was even looking forward to specific summit days in February. Charlie also had a subtheory about flight patterns. He was convinced that commercial pilots would fly over the Fitzroy range in stable weather.

Two other Americans showed up and had us searching for low-flying condors as well, supposedly another sure sign of good weather. With days upon days of free time to kill, the American flight theories took discouragingly little time to research—we usually couldn't even see the sky.

The two Swiss climbers sharing the hut with us were firm disciples of the barometer. Until their altimeter-barometers showed high pressure, they weren't budging a single meter. Charlie made no effort to disguise his scorn for what he called "altimeter paralysis."

"Barometers only tell you what the weather's doing right now," he'd say disdainfully. "Besides, if the barometer says it's good and you're still down at base camp, you're already too late."

Poincenot and Fitzroy (photo by Heinz Zak)

I agreed with Charlie, and we did manage to climb a couple more routes. But the most impressive result of our philosophy was an intensely intimate knowledge of the route across the glacier to our high bivy. We also provided endless entertainment for the Swiss, who were laughing more or less openly at our tendency to rush up to our bivy at the drop of a sunbeam. They would look up from their tea when we'd straggle into the hut, drenched to the skin from yet another lost gamble across the glacier. Without a word, they'd glance significantly at their altimeters and shake their heads.

By the end of January, our standards for good climbing weather had sunk so low that we started up the Aiguille de l'S—"It's the smallest, easiest mountain around," Charlie said—in a gentle snow, reasoning that at least it wasn't windy. Not long after, we turned back in a full blizzard and counted the day as exercise.

The storm ended in an abrupt calm: no wind, no clouds, planes streaming across the sky, condors flying. If we'd had an altimeter, it would have read "summit." In shock, we started up toward the S again, already planning our next routes.

When we climbed out of the snow gully to the shoulder of the S, the first shadow of doubt crept in. The first pitch was more snow than rock, and we were climbing in mountain boots. We popped over the ridge to see snow-coated granite blazing white in the sun. Clearly none of the rock on the peaks was going to be climbable today, or even tomorrow. "The smallest, easiest mountain around" loomed larger and out of reach.

"I can't believe this season is so bad," Charlie said. "I soloed a new route on the S last year, and here we are project-ing the thing." Bitterly disappointed, we turned back.

All around, the snow gleamed blinding white and the sky was bluer than I'd ever imagined. It was a real, live splitter day, and suddenly it didn't even matter that we were slogging down summitless again. I was experiencing a legend, like meeting the Easter Bunny or watching the Red Sea part. I finally believed that good weather existed in Patagonia, and I couldn't wait to start climbing in it.

That night, the wind crept in, and we woke the next morning to blowing sleet. But I had this new theory about wind patterns. . . .

A CRACK IN THE WINDOW

Charlie and I woke the third day in our snow scrape to find ourselves covered in spindrift again. After climbing five thousand feet of rock, snow, and ice up the west side of Fitzroy, and with only two thousand feet of granite between us and the summit, we wanted to stay put. But our fuel bottle was almost empty and we had just a few cookies and candy bars left. We'd lost our gamble on the weather for the umpteenth time in our two and a half months in Patagonia.

The storm was still raging after we'd laboriously packed, so we hunched in the disintegrating snow cave and ate the last of our food. At 11:00 AM, it was now or never, and we set off down the first snowfields to the serac. The ice wasn't hard enough to hold an ice screw, so we chopped big, bulbous bollards into the stiff snow, torso-size bas-relief sculptures with a deep groove in the back to drape the rope over.

As Charlie rappeled from the third bollard, I squeezed my eyes shut against the stinging needles of sleet and opened them to see a ropeless bollard. I wiped my eyes clear and looked again. The ropes were still gone. It didn't make sense; the bollard was grooved so deeply, there was no way they could have popped off, and I'd only shut my eyes for seconds. I would have seen the ropes sliding if one end had started to pull. I leaned over the bulging ice, trying to see through the flying snow. Far below, the edge of the serac jutted out, forming a vertical ice pitch above a snow basin. I yelled into the wind, listening to my voice tear away.

It struck me that Charlie was either dead or very far below with the ropes. Somehow it was too unreal to be very upsetting. I wondered with calm detachment how I was going to downclimb the steep ice pitch below these ice slabs, not to mention the other thousands of feet of snow and rock. I didn't know I if could, but my other choice was to stay on this ice ledge partway up Fitzroy.

OPPOSITE: Attempting to summit Fitzroy via the American Route, 1997 (photo by Charlie Fowler)

I took a deep breath, twisted my ice tool leashes securely around my wrists, and firmly kicked my crampon points into the ice. After about twenty methodical steps, I suddenly heard my name rip past on the wind. I stopped, trying to decide if it was real, and then it came again. I switched directions, slamming my tools in hard, until I reached the ledge, numbly waiting until I heard the *chink chink* of Charlie's tools. He reached my stance, and after a confused second I saw the ropes behind him.

"I stopped at a ledge," he shouted through the roar, "and the wind picked the ropes off the bollard. I caught them, but I knew what you'd be thinking. I got back up as fast as I could."

Still numb, I grabbed him in a hug.

The storm worsened as we continued our rappels, and I became sure that I never would have made it down alone without a rope. The wind was now so fierce that we had to belay each other on the low-angle snow below the serac, dropping to our knees when big gusts tore in. Ice balls pelted us from above, accompanied by showers of snow that avalanched down one minute and blew straight up the next.

At last, after countless rappels and twelve hours of battling the storm, we were off Fitzroy, just as dusk fell. Suddenly the drama was over and we were slipping over snow-covered boulders in our mountain boots. Now that the fear of death was past, I felt irrationally angry at Patagonia and sick of fighting the weather. I stumbled and slid, blinking back tears of rage. Finally, I fell hard and sprawled in the talus. Charlie stopped behind me.

"I hate this place!" I burst out. "We almost died all day! Half of our friends showed up three months ago in perfect weather and climbed everything and we've been working like dogs and we lose every gamble and I've never even seen one day of decent weather and I'm sick of it! I've had it, Charlie. This is it. I'm going down tomorrow."

"Yeah, I've had it right now too," he said.

The tiny bivy tent was like a luxury palace, dry and full of food. We woke to a clear day and watched the wind dwindle as our wet clothes dried. It was unbelievable, but the weather finally seemed to be changing. Looking up at Fitzroy in the bright blue sky, I had a hard time equating it with the mountain that had so ferociously herded us down just twelve hours ago. I suddenly heard myself say, "You know, Charlie, if we go up again it'll be so much easier. We know the way, all the anchors are fixed, and it could never be that bad again."

Charlie's immediate laugh was almost a relief—until I turned to see him repacking his gear.

4

OPENING OUT

The disciple should hunger for knowledge and have the spirit of
humility, perseverance, and tenacity of purpose.
—B. K. S. Iyengar

CLIMBING IN PATAGONIA BLEW MY MIND. Nothing I had ever done prepared me for what it was like to fight those storms. After I returned from my first trip there, my boyfriend Kennan invited me on a trip to Kyrgyzstan. A Patagonia veteran himself, he didn't need my letters home to understand how maddening my stormy trip had been. He promised that Kyrgyzstan was sunny, in fact, was known for having the best, most stable weather imaginable. It would be a trip of Asian travel and sunny granite peaks, all free climbing. It sounded great. We would be a group of six, off for summer adventure.

That April, in preparation, I climbed the Nose in Yosemite with two guys I had known for a few years. I may as well confess once and for all that I have a horrible memory for names and even faces, which only seems to be getting worse. I even forget people I have traveled with! This is disturbing, and Dean teases me mercilessly. So when I can't remember a person's name, ridiculous as it seems, I call them Joe. Or Mike. Maybe no one will notice.

Joe, Mike, and I wanted to climb the Nose wall-style, but we agreed that we would all free climb as much as we could, instead of aid climb, since most of the route is of moderate difficulty, with only short crux sections. When we got to the first crux, the Great Roof, its traversing nature made it impractical for more than one person to free climb be-

OPPOSITE: Below Peak 4520, Kyrgyzstan (photo by Kennan Harvey)

cause of the need for directional gear on the sideways-running rope. Joe and I were both curious to check it out. Mike generously volunteered to aid up it with the rope, and then Joe and I were left to come up afterward—one of us would get to try free climbing the pitch on toprope, the other would have to jug, using ascenders to climb the rope in an efficient but less interesting stair-step motion. I was stunned when Joe informed me that he should climb the pitch and I should jumar because he was more qualified.

"How many 5.13 pitches have you climbed?" he demanded. I was dumbfounded. I wasn't going to argue so I let Joe have his chance, but fumed as I jumared the line, asking myself if I should have brought a climbing résumé up El Capitan. Later on the route, he made disparaging comments about the trip I was dreaming of—to go the following year to the Karakorum with a group of women friends. We were all so inexperienced, we would surely get an altitude spanking, he told me. Joe and I had known each other for a fairly long time, and I was confused and angered by his condescending attitude, which I had never glimpsed during our fun crag days in the past. The mounting tension made the climb rather torturous, for all of us, even the easygoing Mike.

Afterward, I questioned the wisdom of my summer plans. The startling Nose experience made me see that going on a foreign trip with a big group, with the possibility of unimagined personality conflicts, could be a recipe for disaster.

Fortunately the Kyrgyzstan trip worked out fine, but over the years I encountered conflicting attitudes toward me as a young woman climber. For a long time I felt that I was often figuratively patted on the head—excessively praised for things that weren't really all that impressive, by real climbing standards, just because I was a decent-looking girl. But at other times, when I did do a particularly good climb, I sometimes encountered a surprising degree of negativity. It was as if there was a certain place for me as a woman, although it took a long time for me to figure that out. Looking nice in pictures and climbing at a high but not threatening level were fine. As I started to push myself harder, things changed. Sometimes the change was subtle, sometimes not. Mostly I felt free to be myself among a respectful, caring community of climbers. But as I began achieving bigger things, I was sometimes baffled by unexpected criticism or belittlement. It's easy to say "sticks and stones, blah blah blah," but the fact is, words can hurt.

As with the other difficult moments in my life, those experiences reinforced the fact that I climb for myself and no one else. Sometimes the distinctions get blurred, and it's easy to get sucked into other people's realities. In the end, climbing is what I love, my own expression of joy. Everything else is just noise.

IN THE LAND OF KYRGYZSTAN

PLANNING

I'd barely heard of Kyrgyzstan, didn't even know where it was until we got there. But after a storm-filled season in Patagonia, it took only the words "Good weather! Big granite peaks!" to get me packing my bags.

The trip to the new republic, bordering northwestern China and once part of the Soviet Union, was complicated from the start. Assembling the team took on all of the drama and complexity of planning a high-school dance. Topher and his girlfriend Patience had organized the trip, so they were definitely going. Kennan, my boyfriend, seemed to want to go but was waiting to see if I'd go. I, of course, wasn't going unless he was. The other issue was Kennan and Topher's tradition of partnership, which was being disturbed by this relatively recent girlfriend situation for both. That, coupled with Patience's lingering elbow tendonitis, made me confused about who my climbing partner would be. No one really seemed sure. There was a vague and general feeling that if no one decided anything, it would all work out once we got there.

I thought I'd solved the problem by asking our friend Doug to come along, until Patience and Topher suddenly announced that they were both injury-free and would be climbing only together. Doug solved the new problem by inviting another friend, Jimmy. Chaos was held in check, if just barely. I began to think it might be best to go with the flow on this trip, a suspicion reinforced when we tried to leave the States.

Kennan and I found ourselves four days behind the rest of the crew, because our airline couldn't get us from Salt Lake City to New York. When we finally landed in Uzbekistan, at the dilapidated Tashkent airport that was in the process of being either renovated or demolished, we were relieved to learn that Topher and Patience had also been delayed and were here as well. Doug and Jimmy were already in the mountains, and the remaining four of us hoped to find them at base camp in about four more days. The journey was starting to seem more like an Asian travel adventure than a climbing trip.

DRIVING

We were driving, sort of, up a long and winding hill on the way to Katran, one of the last towns before our goal, the towers rising above the Ak-Su Valley. The boxy minivan didn't like carrying six people with expedition gear and food up steep passes. Travel was slow. The land was big and arid. In our frequent stops to tend the radiator, I observed the scruffy goats and donkeys and the women selling melons, honey, and sour milkballs along the roadside. The women wore gauzy dresses shot with multicolored metallic threads, and filmy, sparkly scarves on their hair. I immediately wanted a sparkly scarf.

A canvas yurt perched on a slope beside the dirt highway. A small boy had been sent down to the road to fetch water from a pipe sticking out of the hillside. A ragged girl and her naked baby brother watched close by.

Semetei was our interpreter, guide, and cook. He was nineteen, toothy, and eager and would start attending the university in Bishkek, Kyrgyzstan's capital, after this trip. His English burst forth in quick phrases, strongly accented and interrupted by hesitations. The van jolted. I asked Semetei if he'd ever been to the Ak-Su Valley. No. I asked what kind of food he usually cooked. He admitted to never actually working as a cook before. In fact, he'd never slept outside, he told me, laughing cheerfully.

Heavy machinery sat idle by the roadside as cars and trucks steadily rolled on. Occasionally we passed a rundown trailer fronted by a table displaying the ubiquitous Fanta bottles and milkballs, presumably for sale. Small children peeked through faded curtains, but their parents never emerged as we rattled past. Kennan spotted a police car coming and asked Semetei if the police often stopped drivers on this road. Semetei answered cryptically, "Some people give money, then there is no trouble. Our driver has given money twice today." The driver did appear rather tense. Semetei remarked that the minivan was not permitted on this road, but he couldn't explain why. We tried to look nonchalant as the police car passed.

Evidently this was a twelve-hour drive, perhaps not counting radiator stops, although it should take only half that time to drive from Tashkent to Katran. But Tajikistan pokes into Uzbekistan like an unfriendly porcupine, blocking a direct route to Kyrgyzstan. The Tajiks had been at civil war for years. Semetei and the driver looked aghast when I asked why we couldn't just drive straight through Tajikistan. Semetei made vague and ominous references to guns and Tajiks. He fired off an alarmed stream of Russian at the driver. I stopped asking questions.

TREKKING

The trail was steep and rocky. We were hot. The Kyrgyz horsemen were wearing the national hat—tall white felt wool with a black velvet brim and filigree patterns stitched on front and back. I immediately wanted a Kyrgyz hat. Torn, navy blue Adidas warm-up pants completed the look. I walked behind a horse, watching the horseman's rubber flip-flops slide as he pulled on the frayed bridle. I asked Semetei why we needed seven men to lead seven horses on this three-day trek. He looked at me in surprise. "They will not trust their horse to another man. Horses are valuable. Forty dollars is how much they can earn in one year."

I felt a bit cheated. Couldn't we pay one man three or four years' salary to lead all the horses, and tip out their owners?

As night fell we laid out our blankets and sleeping bags, then sat in a circle with the horsemen. They produced a plastic soda bottle of champagne-colored wine that tasted of apples. We talked through Semetei as the wine went around.

"How old are you?" they asked me.

"Twenty-five."

"You have children?"

"No!!" We all snickered. The horsemen looked puzzled.

"You and Kennan are married?"

"No!!"

Most of the horsemen were about my age, and all of them had at least three children. They were curious about our jobs. They assumed we were rich. I'd never earned more than seven thousand dollars a year, which was below poverty line in the States. But maybe I was?

The next day we stopped at noon. Semetei was exhausted. He'd never walked this much in his life, and he looked a bit bedraggled from his first night on the ground. Only after we had tea and packed all the bags were we able to pry him from his sleeping bag in the morning. I sat in the shade beside a nomad hut, tentatively touching my tongue to a dried sour milkball an old woman had given me. It was dingy, rock hard, and smelled faintly of horse manure. They were supposed to satisfy thirst. I couldn't see these things satisfying anything except a desire to throw them away. I slipped it into my bag, smiling appreciatively as though I planned to savor it later. Kennan hucked his into a bush when the nomad woman wasn't looking.

Semetei and Topher were watching the horsemen. All seven of them had been drinking yogurt and tea at a distant hut for almost two hours now. The packs and bags lay beside the horses in a large meadow. Perhaps the men were discussing improved strapping techniques, I thought optimistically. The baggage had been falling off the horses regularly for the entire trip. "They look like a bunch of construction workers on strike," Kennan observed.

Kyrgyz horsemen and their hats (photo by Kennan Harvey)

Semetei went over to investigate. The horsemen were indeed on strike. They wanted more money. Topher looked around the nomad settlement. "They might have the right idea with the strike," he said dryly, "but they probably shouldn't have decided to do it in a field full of other horses. I bet these nomads wouldn't mind earning a year's salary."

Semetei got worked up. He took his job seriously. As he shouted at Serohzdeen, the chief horsemen, his face reddened and saliva sprayed from his lips. The horsemen crouched on the ground nearby, listening intently. I saw their eyes tighten as I tried to help Topher and Kennan negotiate, and I looked at them in equal disgust. Twenty minutes earlier one man had seen me take a bottle of ibuprofen from my pack. He had pointed to his head and grimaced, then pointed at the medicine. The other six had suddenly developed headaches too, and I'd reluctantly passed out most of my only bottle. Now, after accepting my gift, they were turning on us.

What about last night's wine drinking and chatting? What about our agreement? I felt betrayed. I walked away as Semetei and Serohzdeen shouted. Kennan gestured and joked with the horsemen as though nothing was happening. For the first time I realized how delicate this trip was. In five minutes we could find ourselves stuck in this remote place, equally far from our destination and our starting point with far more baggage than we could carry.

DESCENDING

Kennan and I climbed to the summit of Peak 3850, "The Center Pyramid." From start to finish, we'd left nothing on the route but some urine and four bolts, avoiding the crux aid pitch and free climbing the whole thing. To us, making the free ascent of the rock face rather than pulling on gear to get through difficult sections, as the first-ascent team had done, was a real prize. Yesterday Kennan had found a short slab traverse that led into a good crack system, and it was the key to freeing the route. We realized today that my last lead was the final aid pitch marked on the topo. We savored the satisfaction of having freed the route as we cruised over easy terrain to the top.

The weather was still perfect ("six hours of rain in forty-two days," Kennan would enjoy repeating to friends when we got home), and the lichen-covered granite glowed in the afternoon sun. The summit ridge was in sight, and all we needed to do was get down before dark. Soon we were greeted by what appeared to be a piece of laundry line looped around a horn. Far below, a loose gully wound tortuously down the back of the peak. We looked into it with distaste. "We could scramble farther along the ridge and check out the other end," Kennan suggested optimistically.

I looked down again. I didn't want to traverse the length of the ridge only to realize we needed to come back. Someone had rapped from here before and presumably made it to the ground. "Let's just go down," I replied.

The gully was gravelly and treacherous, a hideous descent route. I held my breath as we pulled each rap line, waiting for it to get stuck in loose blocks and to pull them down on us. Stones came hurtling down sporadically as we crept over loose, wet scree between rappels. I felt like a pin in a bowling alley, and I also felt silly rapping the sections that weren't all that steep. But the idea of scrambling unroped down the gravel-covered shelves was horrifying. It wasn't difficult terrain, but it would be all too easy to skate on a gravelly step and fall hundreds of feet down the gully. I resigned myself to being tense and totally gripped. Annoyingly, Kennan didn't seem bothered and didn't even say "I told you so."

As night fell, we reached a cliff at the bottom of the gully. We rapped into the dark, swinging in to place nut anchors in fractured rock. It was a relief to reach the talus and coil our ropes. We picked and slid down, forded the river, and arrived at camp. "I guess it was the wrong way," I said sheepishly.

The next day Doug and Jimmy returned from climbing Russian Tower, the peak beside ours. With shudders they recounted their descent. Their topo encouraged them to rappel near a water streak. Despite their better judgment, they did and ended up setting fifteen anchors, leaving most of their climbing gear. It took them almost as long to get down as it did to climb the route. Evidently it was the wrong water streak. Before Russian Tower, they'd climbed Asan Peak in the neighboring Kara-Su Valley. That descent had taken them down a death gully that randomly loosed showers of blocks around them. Purely by chance they hadn't been hit.

So far everyone had returned from their climbs bearing horror stories of epic descents. Our topos in French and Russian, with vague line drawings, mainly served to lead us astray. Doug and I began to reminisce fondly about Patagonian descents, doing countless rappels down the same routes we climbed up, fearing only stuck ropes, failed anchors, and storms.

A week later Topher and Patience climbed Peak 3850. Sufficiently dissuaded by our tales of the gully, they went to the other end of the ridge and made a few raps to a pleasant grassy slope, which they strolled down. I glanced at Kennan apologetically.

SOCIALIZING

Sometimes it was too hot at base camp, other times we huddled by the fire. A constant stream of local nomad hunters occupied the plank benches around the cook site. They brought their own bread and yogurt and drank tea for hours with Backet, our new cook. Semetei was in Bishkek starting his first semester, probably impressing girls with tales of mountain adventures and crazy American climbers. On his last four days he hiked about ninety miles to bring messages and to prepare for Backet's arrival and Doug and Jimmy's early departure. His month in the mountains turned him into a ridiculously strong hiker, mostly thanks to his preference for carrying messages and buying bread from the locals rather than cooking anything.

Backet was older and knew much less English. He did, however, know how to cook—and even, on occasion, wanted to. The locals liked him more than Semetei, and they lingered around camp regularly. Sometimes two or three days went by before they left. I wondered if their families noticed their absence. Not much hunting seemed to happen. What could be so exciting in our base camp? "I think they just like to get out of the house," Kennan said.

I got tired of trying to communicate with Backet. It was hard work. Someone somewhere had taught him to say "little little" instead of "very little," and as this was one of his few English phrases, it wasn't long before I felt like I was in a Little Caesars pizza commercial. Kennan had endless patience for breaching the language barrier. When he talked to the Kiwi trekkers who passed through, he said "mate" and "glay-see-er." When he talked to the British climbers, he said "abseil" instead of "rappel," meeting the passersby in their own idiom. He was indefatigably flexible. He spent hours with Backet, triumphantly deciphering one piece of news. When we checked the information with a local who spoke English, the news was totally wrong.

Today Kennan was engaged in another elaborate discussion with Backet. He pointed to imaginary donkeys. "One *ishik,* two *ishik,* three *ishik,* four *ishik.* Everybody happy!" Kennan repeated this several times while Backet thumbed through a Russian–English dictionary. I wondered if we would ever see the donkeys.

The Kyrgyz visitors noticed my interest in their bread making. Backet broke off from the donkey discussion to point at me and announce, "Bread study!"

The young men smiled at me encouragingly from the fireside. One boy held his hands out and another poured water over them. He put a few inches of water into our red plastic bowl, dropped in two lumps each of salt and soda, and stirred with his finger. Then he reached into the flour sack with cupped hands and added two loads of flour. As he started mixing with his hands, Backet leaned over to tell me, "Two breads." The other men sat in the shade and pointed to me, wanting me to take a turn kneading. I shook my head.

"His bread," I said firmly. Wouldn't want to cause trouble in the kitchen.

The bread maker kneaded for almost ten minutes until the dough was as white as plaster. He called for more water and dipped his hands in it, punching wet fists into the dough over and over. As the iron pot heated, he rubbed a piece of goat fat around the bottom and added some sticks to the fire. He pressed the dough flat, punched holes in the top with a twig, and laid it in the pot.

We all smiled at each other and waited for the bread to brown. It turned out crusty and chewy. I was impressed that the men made their own bread.

That night a hunter offered Kennan some of the green powder we'd seen them chewing. It smelled like dried pond algae. Gamely, Kennan put a pinch in his lower lip while Topher, Patience, and I goggled at him and questioned him on his state every thirty seconds. He started to get a head rush and a burning lip, and quickly spat the stuff out.

"No throwing up," I said sternly.

Patience observed Kennan's face. "You're not a very good color," she said.

"You do look a bit haggard," I observed.

"I don't *feel* nauseous though," Kennan said suddenly, and then lunged past me and vomited into a bush. We all looked at each other in shock but were unable to stop laughing hysterically. Between heaves, Kennan laughed too. The Kyrgyz men watched us inscrutably and tucked more powder into their lips.

ON MY OWN

My alarm rang at 3:30 AM, but I was already wide awake in my sleeping bag, pummeled by doubts. My backpack was ready and waiting outside, my stash of ropes and water was up at the base of Peak 4520, and I was trying to remind myself why on earth I wanted to go up there alone.

In the last three weeks I'd climbed five peaks with Kennan, but I was dissatisfied. It wasn't that Kennan was a bad partner; actually, he was too good. I craved the uncertainty of knowing that success or failure was entirely up to me. Peak 4520, grandly nicknamed "A Thousand Years of Christianity in Russia," sat insistently above our base camp in the Pamir-Alai of Kyrgyzstan. It was one of the Ak-Su Valley's two major granite towers that I hadn't yet climbed. The idea of soloing 4520 had crept into my mind, and I couldn't get it out.

From camp, the best route on this side of 4520 was obvious. It cruised up the right shoulder and then followed beautiful crack systems to the summit. Two other parties in our group had already climbed it, taking three days and a day and a half, respectively. I knew it had about thirty sixty-meter pitches, with mostly 5.8 and 5.9 climbing and a little 5.10. It was well within my ability but difficult enough that I wouldn't want to free solo without ropes. I was shy of running around camp announcing that I planned to solo the route, so I didn't have much more specific information. The longest thing I'd ever soloed was five pitches, and I'd only rope-soloed, self-belaying, for two pitches before. I was scared of bad weather. I was scared I might not make it to the good bivy ledge before dark. I was scared of failure. Mostly I was scared to get out of my sleeping bag, because I knew that once I left I wouldn't have anyone to spur me on.

I slipped out into the dark and grabbed a handful of raisins. Heading out of camp and up a rocky slope, I found the easy pillar I'd gone up the day before and began to climb, remembering early morning scrambles up the North Chimney on Longs Peak. When I reached my stash of ropes and water, it was still dark and cold, and I was at the end of familiar ground. It felt oddly quiet without someone to talk to. I flaked the ropes and loaded my pack with six liters of water.

Dawn was breaking. After several hundred feet of easy climbing, I put myself on belay. I'd never soloed with a Grigri before, but the modern autolocking device seemed better than using the old-school knot system I knew of. I had to laugh at myself for improvising my systems partway up a peak in the middle of Kyrgyzstan. Still, I quickly got into the rhythm of leading each pitch, making an anchor, switching the Grigri to rappel, slapping the ascenders on the rope, and going back up with the pack. The routefinding demanded more attention. I had a tiny, vague topo with French alpine ratings that didn't mean much to me, and I was in a sea of granite littered with cracks and tiny roofs. As the pitches rolled by, I glanced at my watch constantly, amazed at how the hours were flying past.

By 4:00 PM, I was still six or eight pitches from the bivy ledge, and I was moving slower. I'd been going since 4:30 AM, and repeating each pitch on jumars with my pack was starting to wear me out. I ate some beef jerky as I placed an anchor and reminded myself to keep a steady pace. I had four hours of remaining light. It was going to be close. I tried for a minute to add up how many pitches I'd done, but it was a jumble. Bits of Bob Dylan songs ran through my head.

I climbed the last few feet to the bivy ledge as dusk was falling. I'd made my goal, after fifteen hours of climbing. I was exhausted, and it was getting cold quickly. I layered up and flaked out the ropes for sleeping. For some reason, food seemed totally unappealing, but I forced down a cheese sandwich and drank a liter of water. Then I put my legs into my pack and got into the bivy sack. It felt like a blast freezer was aimed into the breathing hole, and for the first time I wished I had a partner or a sleeping bag. I'd forgotten gloves, so I put my extra socks on my hands, stuck a liter of water in my sack, and began a long night of impersonating a hedgehog. As I shivered, I thought over the day's work and realized with a start that I'd climbed, rappeled, and jugged at least twenty pitches.

At 6:30 AM, I gratefully gave up the pretense of sleeping. A thin layer of frost coated my rock shoes, and I cursed myself for leaving them out. Feeling like Cinderella's wicked stepsister, I forced them on. To save weight, I stashed two liters of water on the ledge. I was tempted to leave the whole pack, but I didn't want to make a stupid mistake. Unlike Yosemite Valley, a mistake here wouldn't result in rangers shouting "Climber, do you need rescue?"

The sun hit quickly this high on the route, and I began to thaw. When the climbing steepened I could sense that the top was near. I finished a beautiful five-hundred-foot dihedral and pulled around a roof fringed with thick icicles, and the summit popped into view. For the first time, I let myself feel impatient with my system of having to rap back down and clean the pitch before jugging back up to start the next one. I was forcefully reminded of my solitude. Talking out loud to myself was beginning to feel normal, though.

At the last ledge, I left everything and climbed unfettered up a sharp ridge to the top. There I was, on the summit, alone. I could see into the neighboring Kara-Su Valley and down onto the tops of all the other towers I'd climbed. It seemed I should sit there and think poetic thoughts or revel in my good luck, but I was getting cold. I downclimbed to my gear and began rappeling.

Two hours later, I reached the bivy ledge, with no desire to spend another cold night there. I had a topo of the descent route, and I could see the line below me. A lower bivy would be a warmer bivy, so I kept rapping, resolving that if I made it to the last gully before dusk I'd keep going. I'd done that part of the descent three weeks earlier, after climbing a small neighboring peak with Kennan. I remembered doing about six rappels and figured I had a chance of finding our anchors in the dark.

The rapping became monotonous. I untangled the ropes for the millionth time and wished yet again that I hadn't sacrificed thicker ropes to save weight. The 7 millimeter snarled into a yarn ball every time it left my hands, and the 9 millimeter wasn't much better. I was spending at least ten minutes dealing with the mess on every rap, yet to my amazement, I remained patient. Normally I would have been swearing at the ropes and threatening to cut them, even if just in my mind. But I'd been in a strangely methodical state for the last two days. I wasn't trying to figure out how to trick my partner into dealing with the tangles, or gallantly offering to take care of them. The team dynamics were simple—all jobs were my jobs.

Darkness fell and my pace slowed to a crawl. Finally I touched ground. Only an hour or so of scrambling, plus one more rappel over a drop-off, and I'd be back in my tent. I estimated gleefully that I'd be asleep by midnight and began to allow myself to think about a warm sleeping bag.

I started down the talus, trying unsuccessfully to conjure a mental map of the landscape. I decided to just keep heading down and to react to each obstacle as it came into the circle of light from my headlamp.

I butt-scooted down some slabs, trying to ignore the nagging feeling that I hadn't done this before, until suddenly the slabs cliffed out. Oh no, I thought, I am so lost. I'm not even oriented enough to be disoriented.

I wasn't going back up the slabs, though. I was too tired, and I had no idea which way to go if I did backtrack. Instead, I looped a sling around a constriction between two giant boulders and rapped to the lip of a big roof. With a sinking feeling, I scanned the rock around me and found no cracks or horns to sling. I could vaguely see ground below, but the ropes felt like they were hanging above it. I pulled them up and gave a toss, listening for a *thwack*. The ropes snapped tight. That wasn't the answer I was looking for, but I was not going back up now.

"Oh well," I said out loud, and rapped over the edge of the roof. By some miracle, the ropes were dangling just above a ledge with a perfect horn, and I could see the ground within another rope length.

I could hear the river at the bottom of the valley, and it spurred me on as I picked my way down the talus. Down, down, down. I started hearing the Talking Heads in my mind, "Take me to the river. . . . " My watch beeped: midnight. Almost there. And then, unbelievably, the ground leveled and sand squished under my shoes.

I stood paralyzed in front of the water, unable to decide which way to head for base camp. Part of me wanted to dash madly in either direction, and part of me wanted to stand there until it got light. All of me wanted to be in my sleeping bag.

Everything I'd done in the last two days suddenly dropped down on me. After all the years I'd spent as a climber, trying to get away from being judged as a young woman, I realized I'd been judging myself that way. Before we left home, I had been uncomfortable with the idea of climbing as Kennan's girlfriend and partner, rather than being on the trip as just another team member. For the last several climbs, my insecurities had whispered that our mutual successes had been due to his abilities.

Now, at the end of my trial, I saw the foolishness of that reasoning. I had succeeded on the route, and much of my success had come from my ability and desire. But I was in the mountains, and despite the unusually good weather here I could easily have failed due to circumstances beyond my control. Getting a rope stuck high on Peak 4520 would not have meant I was an incompetent climber; it would have meant I'd had some bad luck.

Standing at the riverbank, I saw that this climb was its own experience. Instead of trying to attach too much meaning to it, I decided to accept it for the adventure it was. Deeply satisfied, I promised to be gentler with myself in the future.

I could see the outline of the Russian Tower in the dark, and I knew which way to go. I started upriver. The path took a familiar bend, and the tents glowed yellow through the darkness.

Finding a rest on the Chouinard-Herbert, Yosemite (photo by Jimmy Chin)

5

JOY AT SUDDEN DISAPPOINTMENT

Whatever comes, comes from a need, a sore distress, a hurting want.
And every need brings in what's needed. Pain bears its cure like a child.
Someone once asked a great sheikh what Sufism was.
"The feeling of joy when sudden disappointment comes."
Don't grieve for what doesn't come. Some things that don't happen
keep disasters from happening.
—Rumi

AS MY FREE CLIMBING ABILITIES IMPROVED, I realized that I was lacking advanced big-wall and aid climbing skills. I had learned enough about big-wall techniques—hauling, jumaring up ropes, aid climbing up gear instead of the rock, and sleeping on the wall—to be able to manage on moderate wall routes. But there is a world of difference between moderate big walling and what wall veterans call hard aid.

On Shipton Spire in Pakistan, I found that experience with more advanced aid techniques could be very necessary for establishing new routes, even on free climbing projects. So I decided to turn my energy into learning more about aid, at least for a year or so. Switching gears like this, even within such a specialized sport, opened me up to a whole new world. I learned a lasting lesson: it's important to keep it fresh, to step into new situations where I have a lot to learn. Not only does this keep up my motivation, but it makes me a better climber. It also puts me into different places, among more diverse groups of people.

Climbing, like any high-focus discipline, requires a special mindset. For years I followed my drive, immune to anything that might sidetrack me from a ravenous need to learn more, climb more, do more. It can be nearly impossible to have a relationship with a person like that. Read any classic mountaineering book and you'll find tales of selfish mountaineers leaving behind good, brokenhearted women as they go off to suffer and/or die on some godforsaken peak. Maybe this is a little melodramatic, but there is always truth in clichés.

Though climbing can be hell on a love relationship, it offers an unparalleled sense of community. And climbing partnerships can forge incredibly intricate bonds between seemingly unlikely people. I'm starting to think that what I climb isn't always as important as how I feel climbing it, or the experience I have. I'm sure that when I look back as an old woman, I'll be seeing these moments through wiser eyes.

One thing that's never changed is my certainty that love means total support of my loved one's passion, whatever it may be. Having been on both sides of the equation, I have found this to be easier said than done. Being a driven person is hard. Being in love with that person can be even harder.

DEEP COLD

I stand in the open phone booth at the edge of Camp 4, examining my list of overdue phone calls. Uncannily connected to my emotions, my dog Fletch shifts uncomfortably and looks up as I narrow my eyes at a passing ranger, who is obviously looking for unsuspecting climbers to harass. I've spent enough time in the Valley to have learned firsthand that the wild stories are actually all true. Despite the way it may look to an outsider, Yosemite climbers aren't just paranoid miscreants, convinced that the rangers are "the Man." The only sure way to stay out of jail and on the walls is to avoid the rangers completely.

I look back at the list and quickly dial my boyfriend's phone number. It seems strange to be climbing here without him. But he has suddenly decided to put climbing on hold and build a house, with his own two hands. I am awed by his determination and his ability, and part of me wants to stay there and help. But I can't deny my need to climb right now, to be free. I have devoted my whole life to this path, and I can't seem to step off it, for anyone.

"Hey, it's me. Things are good. I really wish you were here though."

"It'll be another year. Maybe two. Who knows."

I sigh. Fletch sits upright expectantly. I catch sight of a tall rangy figure with a thatch of raven-black hair. Dean. He sees us and heads toward the booth. Our eyes meet through the open doorway.

"Kennan," I say into the phone, "can't you just take a little break and come to the Valley for a while?"

Dean's face darkens, and he abruptly vanishes.

I frown, perplexed. Dean and I had sat together for hours in El Cap Meadow the other day, agreeing not to let our past relationship get in the way of being friends, even making vague climbing plans together. It had all felt so amicable and grown up. So why did he just storm off like a jealous boyfriend? How did climbing get so complicated?

Fletcher lies down, head on her paws.

"Listen, Kennan, I'm really proud of you for going for it with the house project. But I have to tell you something. I found this book, and I think it's really important. It's by this Persian poet, about something called Sufism. It's like a philosophy, or a religion. I've never heard of this before, but I think it's actually really well known. But these poems, they make sense to me in every way. I just opened the book randomly and started reading this poem called 'Joy at Sudden Disappointment,' and it seems to clarify everything for me. It's completely amazing. I can't even believe it. Look, it's a couple pages long, but I have to read it to you."

I finish the poem. "What do you think? Don't you love it?"

There is dead silence, then, "When are you coming back to Colorado?"

"Ummm, well," I don't know, exactly. I'd said I would be back weeks ago, but there's always another climb I need to do, and. . . . When I hang up, things feel bad. A lot of me feels like I should be there swinging a hammer with my boyfriend, helping him build his castle. I know he wants it for both of us. My aspirations are more selfish, but freedom means everything to me. I need to be here, climbing, following my own dreams, and I can't let go of them. I don't know how to make everything right. Things seem oddly conflicted now. I look down at my list again. Parents, Grandma, Russel, Lisa, Kim, Virgil.

I wonder why Russ hasn't been in the Valley this month. I punch in my calling-card number.

"Hey, Steph, how's the Valley?"

It's such a relief to talk to someone who's actually happy that I'm climbing.

"It's great," I say. "But it'll be hot soon, I'm sure. Why aren't you around?"

"I'm leaving for Baffin next week."

"Oh God, I've always wanted to go there," I say fervently. "Actually, I'd give anything to be in the middle of the Arctic right now."

Six days later I'm standing in the Ottawa airport with Russ and Joe, a guy I've just met. He's very young and seems pleasant, but it turns out that Russ has never met him before either. I immediately turn to Russ, but he has developed a sudden interest in the departures signboard. A few hesitant questions reveal that Joe has almost no climbing experience. He is, however, the one who planned this whole trip—putting up new routes in the Baffin fjords. For unclear reasons, his partners backed out at the last minute. He somehow tracked down Russ, and now here we all are. I'm more than a little surprised to learn all this. A trip to the most notorious big-wall destination in the world seems a little ambitious for a first expedition, and for a guy with almost no experience. But it seems to be working out well so far. Russ has plenty of experience in Baffin and with hard aid, and I'm quite competent on walls. I'm sure Joe will do fine. The best climbers always take on more than seems plausible. That's how you learn.

From Ottawa we take progressively smaller planes that eventually dump us and our bags onto a snow-covered runway. I look around. It's cold and white. I see one tiny building that must be the airport. Other than that, nothing. We leave our bags in the building and set out along the hard-packed roadway that leads us about a mile into Clyde River. The town is nothing more than lines of ramshackle wooden houses along the road, with some dog pens out a ways in the snow. There are snowmobiles and parts, skins stretched on poles, and lots of scrap things around. I'm still astonished at the white, and all of its different shades. Grayish, bluish, yellowish, but most of all, white. The snow gleams and sparkles and holds more textures than I've ever seen.

I'm wearing my regular down jacket and it feels like a windbreaker. Luckily Russ has brought an extra Arctic-weight hooded down parka. My jacket seems destined to be an underlayer. The cold is one of the things that has intrigued me about Baffin, and I've been thinking about it constantly. Will I be able to survive in such cold? The Inuit are cruising up and down the street on snowmobiles with light jackets on, a few of them gloveless. For them, the frigid air of June is the cusp of high summer. The sun never sets, and in a couple months the snow on the ground will even melt for a few unpleasant, muddy weeks.

We knock on the door of a small house and are welcomed in by Jushua and his wife, Beverly. Jushua is Inuit, Beverly a nonnative who came here from lower Canada. They run a tiny business, carting climbers and adventurers by snowmobile or boat into the fjords. Russ has warned me that they charge outrageously high prices for the service. But it's a two-day trip by sled, being pulled by the snowmobiles, or "skidoos," and it seems like a bargain to me. How else would we ever get in there?

Jushua is short, strong, and brusque, but prone to surprising bursts of hilarity. Beverly is solemn and motherly, with a thick gray-streaked braid down her back. She runs the entire business, managing everything by phone and computer. Jushua seems almost like a wild animal indoors, not completely at ease, passing time. Their kids drift in and out. "They're all on different time schedules," Beverly tells me. Their teenage son stays up all "night" and sleeps all "day." In the twenty-four-hour daylight of Arctic summer, it's all just numbers anyway. Beverly invites us to stay for dinner, and then we are offered the use of a nearby house to organize and pack for the trip.

We spill our bags onto the floor. I'm familiar with the mass amounts of gear needed for aid climbing but am startled when Russ pulls out big bags of hand-ground rivets, tangles of copperheads, and pounds of drill bits. Although my interest in climbing big walls is recent, I've been reared in a strict tradition of "light is right." I'm awed by the hundreds of pounds of gear the devoted aid climbers will haul up El Capitan. Sure, you're hauling and you don't need to hurry. But why get a hernia? I've been plenty comfortable on El Cap without a boom box and two cases of beer.

"Uh, do you want to bring all that?" I ask carefully.

"Yeah, we need it," Russ says.

I am definitely the less experienced one here, having never done a purely aid first ascent, so I just nod and wonder how we are going to carry all this stuff up the wall.

Joe is sitting in the midst of piles of cardboard boxes containing the food he has carefully packed and sent up here in advance. I look at the first box. It's stacked with industrial-size cans of chili. So is the next one and the next one. And the next one.

"Did you send anything besides chili?" I ask.

"Yeah, there's a box of macaroni noodles too."

"Oh," I say. "So, Joe, what routes have you climbed on El Cap?"

"The Zodiac," he replies.

"Oh! That's a great route. Did you spend a few days?"

"Yeah, it took us twelve days."

Russ and I stare at each other. The Zodiac is the easiest and shortest aid route on El Cap, about fifteen hundred feet long. Climbing at a *very* leisurely pace, it should take no longer than four days. Most people do it in two or three. Usually the constant parties of climbers leave pins and other hardware in place, and it can be climbed quickly, without ever having to break out a hammer. A twelve-day ascent really doesn't seem possible and may be a new anti-speed record.

"So, um, what made you decide to plan this trip here to Baffin, to do a first ascent?" I ask.

"I just thought it was the logical next step," Joe says.

"Oh," I say. "And did you have an objective in mind?"

"No."

"Oh."

Russ and I discuss potential routes. Almost all of the climbing in the eastern fjords has been confined to the Sam Ford Fjord, although an American team recently climbed Sail Peak in the Stewart Valley. We talk briefly of going into the Stewart, but then Russ mentions that he has snowmobiled through the distant Gibbs Fjord and that no one has climbed anything in it. If we go to the Gibbs, we risk finding nothing but choss. But the chance of climbing in a totally unexplored Arctic region is irresistible. And this whole trip is already so random that going into the Gibbs seems inevitable.

In two days, we are packed and loaded. Fortunately I brought a decent supply of dehydrated wall food, but we decide to take a box of the chili just in case. We haul our heavy bags out to the front yard, where they sit on the snow next to crude-looking wooden sleds, "komatiks." Joshua hefts the bags up as though they are full of cotton candy and lashes them down. I've packed all the warm clothes I own for this trip, and I'm already wearing them all. I'm starting to think I'm going to freeze. Russ has warned me that the worst part of the trip is leaving the indoors and sitting for days in the open komatiks. This is really it. Tonight we will be sleeping on the ice, leaving the last bit of civilization far behind.

Joshua looks at me stomping my feet and surprises me by saying, "You cold? Those clothes are no good in the Arctic."

Dressing Inuit (Steph Davis collection)

This is not very good news, as I am wearing the most high-tech nylon and down there is. Jushua drops the cord he is tying onto the komatik and disappears. He comes back holding a pair of Wellington boots, hand-sewn snow pants with a sealskin outer layer, and a green cloth jacket. I'm puzzled by the jacket at first. It looks like something

I remember from Chilly Willy the Penguin cartoons, and I can't figure out how to get it on. It is also handmade, with a second inside layer of thick wool felt, but it has no zippers or fasteners. Eventually I realize that I have to pull the whole thing over my head. It's work to squeeze my head through the neck hole, and the hood hugs my face tightly with a tickly fur trim.

"Dog fur," Jushua says. "Doesn't let the snow in."

Once I am bundled into the Inuit clothes, I realize he is absolutely right. I have immediately become warm, for the first time since we got here. Too bad I can hardly move, or these would be great for climbing.

My satisfaction fades instantly when I notice I have to pee. I have three pairs of pants under the sealskin bib, and three layers under my down jacket and the green pullover. This is going to be an epic. I have just discovered the interesting fact that holding it makes me colder, and that isn't an option here. Slightly traumatized, I struggle with my clothes until I peel down enough to make it happen. The whole battle takes at least ten minutes. My mind flicks to the weeks ahead, wondering how I will ever manage to perform this task day after day.

Jushua seems like a different man now that we are loaded and ready to roll. He sits on his snowmobile looking undeniably bad-ass, like a cross between a cowboy and a Harley rider. Although he scoffed at my synthetic clothes, he is wearing a huge expedition parka that a climbing team gave him, along with massive gauntleted gloves and a hat with earflaps. Leaving the town of Clyde, flying over the ice into the Arctic, Jushua exudes the vigorous serenity of an alpha male entering his territory.

I have to remind myself how excited I am to be here throughout the next two days of torturous open-air travel. In the twentieth century, dogs are passé, although the komatiks haven't changed. With no shock absorption or wind protection, they bounce mercilessly and redefine any previous concepts of cold.

Jushua and his two friends are tireless, and they never get cold. But they stop incessantly for skidoo breakdowns and tea breaks. The first time a snowmobile conks out, I'm anxious. What will we do if no one can fix it? Jushua and his two friends stand in front of the open hood, drinking tea and examining the inner workings. After a while, Jushua reaches in and jiggles something. On the next try, the skidoo roars to life. This seems to be a common occurrence, and no one looks too concerned.

Jushua is entertained by my constant questions about polar bears. He tells stories about fighting bears with his bare hands and surviving. He says it's all about facing the bear down and feinting in the right direction, in the end actually diving toward the bear and baffling it. I believe him. I wonder if I could ever manage to survive if a bear comes after me. Russ tells me that even if you shoot a bear, it's so full of fat and muscle that it's likely to continue killing you anyway. They sound terrifying, and I worry about camping on the ice when we reach our destination.

On one tea break Jushua unhooks the komatik from his snowmobile and suddenly tosses me on the back. We go careening far out over the white plateau until I see a cream-colored polar bear running next to us at almost the same pace as the machine. I am in awe, and I try not to wonder when we had the last skidoo breakdown. "A small one," he shouts over the roar of the skidoo, "female." Jesus. If that's a small one, I don't want to see a big one. Jushua chases the bear for several minutes and then opens the throttle and speeds away. I am deeply impressed and instantly stop speculating about how to survive a polar bear attack. One look has shown me that if a polar bear wants to eat me, it will, and there's no point worrying about it. Russ is green with envy when we rejoin the crew. "This is my third time here, and I've never gotten to see a polar bear," he says.

"Well, I have to say, I hope you don't get to. I could be fine not seeing another one."

I'm impressed by the Inuits' blend of stoicism and rowdy humor. Jushua shoots a seal and drags it to the komatik. I look at it—the seal is as round and fat as a giant furry egg, with a rather fierce-looking set of doglike teeth. Jushua kicks it, apparently for the sole purpose of making blood gush from the bullet holes. He looks at my expression and laughs.

"I don't hear no laughing, I only hear crying!" he sings. He seems to get a huge kick out of saying that to us, especially when we are looking particularly hypothermic or wretched.

The Inuit boil up some chunks of seal meat in water and try to convince me to eat it. It's horrible, rubbery, and bland. "You have to eat seal if you want to be warm," Jushua says. I believe him, but I can't do it.

Our first night is comfortable, finally in the familiar environs of my tent and sleeping bag, and I am relieved to sleep warm, although the lack of darkness is hard to get used to.

It's close to evening of our second day in the komatiks when we turn into the Gibbs Fjord, past Scott Island, into unknown territory. Granite appears everywhere. I shake myself from a cryogenic stupor and try to rev my frozen brain into action. What to climb? There are interesting-looking walls unfolding all around us, but how big are they? How good are they? After ponderous days of travel, the trip suddenly hinges on the decision of a moment. Inexplicably, the same Inuit who had spent two days in Clyde getting "ready to leave in an hour" become frantic to get our gear off the sleds and rush home.

We stall as long as we can, trying to get a look at the walls, and then bow to fate and unpack at the base of a monolith reminiscent of Wyoming's Devils Tower, where we have stopped for tea anyway. It has an appealing shape, seems somewhat south facing, looks big, and sits at the confluence of the Gibbs, Clark, and Refuge Harbor Fjords, which has a certain harmonic appeal. Also, we are here. Decision made. Jushua and his friends wish us luck and drive off. Watching the sleds disappear into the distance, I feel very alone. I wonder if they will come back to pick us up in four weeks, as we've agreed.

As I unpack our bags, set up the tents, and start to organize climbing gear, I feel more at home. Soon equipment is spread around the ice, and things take on the familiarity of any other climbing trip. The borrowed rifle sits among the piles of ropes and hardware. I no longer think it will do us much good if a hungry polar bear shows up, but the fat seals that bask next to ice holes all around ease my mind. Surely they would make a better meal than we would.

I stare up at the wall, looking for our line. I can't believe I forgot to bring binoculars or a spotting scope. Russ assures me that he never brings those and shows me how to scope a line in Baffin: we walk a few hundred yards back on the sea ice, look up for forty-five seconds to make sure there is a steep headwall, and then walk back and start humping loads to the base. Silly me. The best line is obviously straight up the middle.

With absolutely no reference points in this huge, wide-open arena, we can't even figure out how big our formation is. I feel strangely safe in this land of soft grays, whites, and blues. Nothing happens fast, and it is all so peaceful and calm. It would be an easy place to die, but I feel inexplicably relaxed here. I announce whimsically that our mission is to measure this wall with sixty-meter ropes, fantasizing about those old expeditions carrying thermometers and compasses up Mont Blanc for the sake of scientific knowledge. Except no one else actually cares how big this thing is, not even other climbers.

Hauling portaledges, aid gear, food, fuel, and ropes to the base takes us several trips and a couple days of slogging up talus slopes. Getting off

Jushua Tower on Baffin Island (photo by Steph Davis)

the ground and onto the wall is always so much work, but we are finally close to launching. I want very much to hang myself on the wall like a food bag in Yosemite, out of reach of hungry bears.

I tease Russ for days about the "aid climbers' route-finding technique" but have to eat my words when the route turns out to be a good line. I'm the designated free climber, and I'm pleased to get to climb bare-handed when warmer temperatures coincide with climbable rock on the lower pitches. The rock is great, vertical and interesting, and steeper regions loom overhead.

The days roll by, almost indistinguishable with no darkness to separate them. It's otherworldly, being on this wall. The sea ice stretches out around us, open and white, comfortingly corralled by granite walls. For some reason the pure, uncomplicated landscape reminds me of the Moab desert, and I feel oddly at home. The portaledges are safe and secure, and we have plenty of fuel. I'm getting used to wearing two down jackets and three hats. It storms almost constantly, but it's gentle storming, just clouds and snow. We're aid climbing anyway, so on stormy days we just put on shell clothing and goggles and slowly press on.

The rock is a type of granite I've never seen before, as hard and smooth as marble. Russ was right to bring an endless supply of drill bits. We have to make our own anchors—we even have to drill rivet ladders through several blank sections—and the unbelievably dense rock blunts and breaks the bits with disturbing regularity. Drilling takes forever. The extreme cold and the increasingly difficult aid keep us moving at a snail's pace, lucky to finish one pitch a day.

From my free climber's perspective, we are creeping upward with the speed of glaciers. I've never experienced a climb before where no one cares how long it takes. But we can't care. The abnormal cold and the slow aid climbing demand pure patience. Drilling an anchor one day, I realize that I've climbed the south face of Washington Column in Yosemite in almost the same time it takes me to hand-drill two holes up here. But then, what does it matter? How can you have an epic when it never gets dark?

We find our routine. We raise the ropes slowly up a few pitches, and then spend a day packing up the ledges and haulbags and hauling

Portaledge camp on Jushua Tower (photo by Steph Davis)

the massive loads as a threesome, needing our combined body weights to move them up the wall. Joe turns out to be completely uneducated about wall systems, and Russ and I take turns coaching him on hauling and rope management. Though our patience is severely tested by Joe's unusual inability to intuit the most basic techniques, we are impressed by his unshakable good nature. We arrange our days around the few hours that the sun hits us on the wall, since it never gets dark. Going to sleep and waking up feels arbitrary, and talking about "days" seems like an anachronism.

For me, this style of climbing is a window onto another world. Although I've done a little bit of harder aid climbing on El Cap, it's not the same thing at all. I interrogate Russ constantly about the new-wave aid ratings, unable to reconcile the traditional El Cap rating system with the system the new aid climbers are using. It appears that the new scale of difficulty is entirely based on the potential for death and dismemberment. There doesn't seem to be any provision in the new ratings for information about how hard the actual climbing is. A1 means it's safe. A2 means it's safe, but you could take a big fall. A3 means it's not safe, and you could take a huge fall. A4 means that if you fall, you will probably die. A5 means that if you fall, you will definitely die, unless some miracle happens. I'm not sure what A6 means. This does not seem like an open-ended system, at least I hope not. Russ is waiting impatiently for the terrain to get more difficult. He is thrilled when he finally gets a pitch that he deems A4. I have no idea how hard my pitches are, because I still don't get it. Is everything A1 unless you fall?

The white quiet invites leisurely contemplation on the nature of time. This trip was so spontaneous that I can't shake the feeling of being in a dream world, maybe not even really here. The open landscape, the dots of seals lounging on the ice below, the languorously drifting clouds, all seem immutable, yet somehow filled with life. I begin to feel love for my nylon portaledge, this little home the size of a cot, hanging on the cold, gray granite. I also start to love the unhurried pace of climbing, the way I have time to gaze out onto the fjords for hours on end. California and Colorado seem far away, like places I know from stories. After three weeks, I've almost forgotten what it was like not to be on this wall, cocooned inside a portaledge fly. I've forgotten what it's like to climb without being swaddled in layers of clothing or standing in stiff plastic boots in ladderlike aiders, tapping and hammering up the swelling wall.

When we finally climb to the summit, walking seems foreign. Russ has brought kites and cigars. I sit for hours, enjoying the rare sunshine, watching long, low clouds creep like dragons along the ice corridors below. This is the first time in three weeks that I've been more than two hundred feet away from Russ and Joe. The day flows by, like they all do.

Two days later, we touch down on the sea ice, once again at the base of the tower that we have started calling Jushua Tower. The ice is melting, and we are anxious as we wait in waterlogged tents for Jushua to come back for us. We are forced to move camp several times, up higher toward the base of the tower, as the ice melts faster. We wonder how the snowmobiles will make it out to us if it keeps up at this rate. Days go by, then Joshua arrives and we are overcome with relief. He seems pleased that we named the tower for him. We ask him several times if the Inuit have a name for it already, but he makes no reply. We bounce out across the watery ice, and Joshua Tower recedes into the distance, into a white memory.

———————|———————

I'm wrapped in the Arctic mist for the entire journey home, content and mellow, but I drive as fast as I can from the Denver airport. Fletcher tears down the gravel road toward my truck. I cry and laugh as I bury my face in her fur, then we dash together around piles of scrap lumber. Kennan sits expressionless as I burst through the door. I look at the pile of empty beer bottles in the trash.

"Did I, um, miss my welcome home party?" I ask uncertainly.

He just looks at me. The air is tense and frigid. "Mike was leaving for a trip to Greenland. We had a going-away party for him last night," he says flatly.

I look at him, stunned. My mind goes as empty as sea ice.

FOUR THOUSAND PULL-UPS

On day three, waking to a hangover and way too many sore muscles, I cling to the portaledge straps unsteadily, leaning against El Capitan.

"Russ, it's your lead."

This may be true, and if it's not, I'm hoping he can't remember either.

Russ looks about as haggard as I do, and luckily shows no signs of being able to discuss whose lead it actually might be, or anything else for that matter. Beth, on the other hand, is rustling around chirpily on her ledge and debating the possibility of doing extra pitches today and maybe topping out tomorrow. I ignore all that. I just want the aspirin. Russ steps into his aiders as I dig through the tangle of ropes and stuff

Aiding up the Zodiac, El Capitan (photo by Kennan Harvey)

sacks heaped on the portaledge. Halfway up the Zodiac, on her first big wall, Beth is doing just fine and appears to be feeling a lot better than me or Russ. Cars loop around the road below us, and we can hear the shouts of nearby parties across the sea of granite.

The constant stress of questioning my own judgment definitely contributed to my need to drink one too many beers last night. Despite having lost the use of her legs, Beth has been wanting to do this climb more than anything, and I am determined to make it happen, but I feel totally responsible for her safety on the wall. Beth is as tough as they get, but only eighteen months after her accident, her body is extremely vulnerable. I've spent most of the route privately worrying about her pain level and potential for injury, asking myself if this climb is a responsible choice. I could tell she was feeling a lot of pain on the first days of the climb but couldn't know if it was just the normal pain of being on a wall or destructive pain. The one thing I do know is that Beth will never be the one to call a retreat, so all I can do is watch her like a hawk and guess at the right decision.

———————|———————

We'd been working toward this ascent since Beth broke her back a year and a half ago in a climbing accident. She had been a favorite Indian Creek partner back in Moab. Our friendship developed as a natural bond between two obsessive female athletes. We'd check in with each other from pay phones to talk about men and upcoming trips, send each other silly postcards, and meet every few months at a sunny crag.

Before I met Beth, she had made a switch from biathlon racing to cross-country mountain bike racing. She had also developed a passion for rock climbing. Beth was remarkably nonchalant, or maybe just humble, about her history as an elite athlete. As time went by, I began to understand just how good she really was.

Beth competed in biathlons in the 1992 and '94 Olympics, as well as in seven World Championships, and then made a seamless move to professional mountain bike racing. She found herself starting at the bottom of her new sport without the sponsorship support that her competitors had acquired. Still, she managed to train and make ends meet, and by 1997 she had earned a national second-place ranking. The mountain biking media loved to run stories about Beth Coats, the underdog blazing to victory, and sponsorships began to roll her way.

On her rest days from training, Beth would go climbing. In three years, she had become a solid leader, dancing up 5.11 routes on gear and 5.12 sport routes. With the unbridled enthusiasm of a new climber, she'd call to tell me about leading every pitch on the Naked Edge in Eldorado Canyon, climbing her first Longs Peak Diamond route, and "Oh yeah I won the race last weekend."

I started to have ideas about doing big routes together some day, but Beth's racing and training schedule was far too intense to indulge in a lot of climbing time. The most she could manage was the occasional half day or weekend at the crag. Her only regret in life was that she didn't have more time to climb, until an afternoon at Eldo when a rock broke under her hand, throwing her down to talus, and she lost the use of all her muscles below her top abdominal muscle—and with them her years of work as a biathlete and mountain biker.

This trip up the Zodiac, the most popular trade route on El Cap, couldn't be more different than the last wall Russ and I climbed together. Two months ago, we were on a new route in Baffin Island, surrounded by nothing but white ice and seals. We climbed in goggles and plastic boots and lived on the wall for weeks.

At the end of the Baffin trip, Russ and I agreed that we could get up any route we needed to together. For years, Beth, an excellent climber with no big-wall experience, had dreamed of doing her first El Cap route. After her devastating accident, and the subsequent months of hospitals and doctors' offices, she badly needed a return to her normal life of adventure, with active friends in wild places. It seemed like the time had come; I knew that with Russ things would run smoothly, and we would all have a really good time.

Mark Wellman pioneered paraplegic climbing over a decade ago when he climbed El Cap, and it is by no means a systemized type of climbing. My friend Timmy had let me tag along on his brother Sean O'Neill's paraplegic ascent of Castleton Tower near Moab the year before, to help out and learn a few things along with them, but neither Russ, Beth, nor I had ever climbed in this style. At a certain point, you just have to start and see what happens.

———————|———————

As we climb, we discover that paraplegic climbing is all about creativity and unexpected glitches. For Russ and me, this El Cap trade route is turning out to be the most technical and demanding wall that either of us have ever been on. Everything has to be done right, with no short-cuts, and in a much more controlled manner than we would normally use. We have to rethink our rope management minutely and rig things to make sure Beth doesn't get stopped by any sort of gear cluster.

We quickly learn that it is not okay for Beth to scrape against the wall on less steep pitches, and we eventually get smart enough to just pull her rope out from the wall and use our bodies as sawhorses to make it hang free while she ascends. Russ and I take turns running extra trips up and down the rope, so that Beth leaves her portaledge to start jugging and then has it waiting for her at the next anchor. It's crucial to make sure she is never hanging in her harness for too long, as that could cause damaging pressure points on her legs. Differences in injury levels that aren't obvious to an outside observer make major differences in techniques and potential problems for a paraplegic climber. Beth has a very high level of injury, with only one functioning abdominal muscle. This alone adds extra effort for her on the wall, as she needs to pull and hold herself upright all the time on the portaledge. She also doesn't have much circulation in her legs, so she is more susceptible to injury.

Beth's harness was custom sewn for her by friends in Moab, and she diligently practiced her jumar system on ski-lift towers at home in Breck-enridge before driving her hand-operated VW van out to the Valley. She has nicknamed her harness, essentially a haulbag sliced in half lengthwise, the "leg burrito." She wears extra-wide leg loops inside it, along with a regular waist harness and a chest harness. To climb a rope, she pushes up her top jumar with a short pull-up bar attached to it, does a pull-up, and

OPPOSITE: Beth Coats jugging up the Zodiac (photo by Steph Davis)

brings up the bottom jumar attached to her harness. When things are going right, she has an efficient rocking motion, leg burrito straight in front of her, gracefully bobbing through the air. On the Zodiac, we figure she will do about four thousand pull-ups, which might sound like an impossible task, if you don't know Beth.

By our third day on the wall, we have all figured out what we are doing and can finally start to relax and enjoy the experience of living on El Cap. This is, after all, the whole point of climbing wall-style. Every time I've told Beth about a wall I've climbed, Beth's first response has been, "Oooohhhh, I want to climb a wall, and sleep on portaledges, and eat food cold out of cans!" Now she is experiencing the joys of cold canned food, at last. Russ thought there was a lot of girl talk to deal with in Baffin, but I was the only girl. Now it's doubled, at least, and I think he's handling it remarkably well. Luckily he's pretty quiet anyway.

Russ and I feel like we have a good system going for the climbing, and Beth no longer seems to be having pain problems. Beth catches on to systems incredibly fast and almost immediately has taken over her share of organization and rope work as we climb. I look down to the parked cars, starting to become visible by El Cap Meadow, and I can see Beth's blue Eurovan with her handbike attached to the back. Around us, other parties are dotted on the Nose, the North American Wall, and Mescalito. Birds swoop past during the temperature changes of early evening. There's no place like this in the world—I know, I've looked. I can't believe we are actually doing this, that we are all on El Cap together, only a year and a half after Beth's accident.

On day five, Beth pulls onto the summit. We throw the gear any which way and gaze at Half Dome in the distance. It seems crazy that we've actually done it, or at least most of it. We still have to get down.

———————|———————

How to get down had posed the most vexing logistical problem during the planning. Initially Beth had her heart set on coming in from Tuolumne to stash her handbike on the trail that leads down from the top of El Cap. She thought if she got piggybacked from the top of Zodiac to her bike, she could ride down the eight-mile trail herself to the

Valley floor. But the Falls Trail is notoriously rough and rocky. It was a great idea but just wouldn't work with a bike. The typical descent, the East Ledges, would definitely be the quickest way down. But the going is steep and treacherous and involves several rappels. Tired and loaded down under heavy haulbags, many climbers epic on the way down. We couldn't afford to do anything sketchy with Beth. We needed the fastest, safest descent plan we could get. I decided that, as with most problems, it could be solved by finding the right people.

Fortunately, Dean and Timmy were climbing together in Yosemite, and they were more than willing to be a part of Beth's climb. Being the biggest, strongest, and fastest climber we know, Dean was elected mule. Timmy became our consultant, thanks to his experience with his brother Sean and their past climbs. Through sheer energy and outrageous personality, Timmy is a perfect ringleader, and he also volunteered to help by spotting Dean, and distracting Beth, as Dean piggybacked her over rough, rocky terrain.

At our systems lab, El Cap Meadow, we cut holes out of the bottom of a Kelty backpack for Beth's legs and then rigged a strapping system to hold her on Dean's back. It turned out something like a humongous kid carrier and worked surprisingly well. Dean and Timmy started us on our climb by ferrying Beth a thousand feet up to the base of the Zodiac in the Kelty. They dropped us off at the Zodiac, promising to watch from the ground and meet us at the top when we were finished. Though we had all discussed the question of the descent route ad nauseam, with plenty of suggestions from interested friends, we had never come to any final conclusions. Dean told us he would think about it and figure out the best plan while we were climbing.

———————+———————

On top of El Cap, happy and exhausted, we make dinner and hang a portaledge in a tree for Beth to sleep in, wondering when Dean and Timmy will show up. I partly expected them to be here when we topped out, but it makes sense that they would want to have an entire day for the descent. I'm sure they must be resting in the Valley, gathering their energy for the challenge.

At dawn, Dean and Timmy arrive with the Kelty, a pack full of orange juice, yogurt, cinnamon rolls, and a whole melon. They casually tell us they would have been here last night, but they were busy finishing a twenty-four-hour linkup of El Cap, Half Dome, and the Sentinel. For most people, climbing any of those formations in one day would be a feat, but Dean and Timmy climbed all three of them! They don't even look tired.

Dean immediately announces that he has figured out the descent plan. The fastest, and therefore safest, descent is directly down the East Ledges, rather than miles and miles down the Falls Trail, he says. I would protest this rather terrifying concept, but I'm too worn out. And by now I've learned that when Dean says he's going to do something impossible, it's best to just stand back, ideally with a camera on hand. Russ and I are happy to load the heavy haulbags onto our backs and turn the reins over to Dean and Timmy's high-octane energy.

For the next three hours, Dean and Beth maneuver down the East Ledges, often at the very edge of El Cap with thousands of feet of exposure below them. They descend through manzanita tunnels, granite slabs, scree, rappels, talus, and then the last stretch of trail through the forest to the Valley floor. Dean moves more like a mountain goat than a mule, and this is the first I've seen Beth looking scared during our entire adventure. Being strapped to the back of a six-foot-six guy descending that sketchy terrain would scare anyone. We all know full well that falling is not an option, which is why we have Dean. Timmy gets to work, entertaining Beth with outlandish tales and his improv narration of "The Dean Potter East Ledges Workout Video."

"Okay, Ladeeeeez," Timmy sings, "grab a ninety-pound paralyzed girl and a rap line! Let's get those ATCs moving! And one and two and come on girls, pass that knot!" Beth is laughing so hard, she forgets that she is clinging to Dean's back, hundreds of feet above the ground, as he slides down a rope.

When we reach the Manure Pile parking lot, Beth's tandem bike is leaned up against a picnic table. Much to her delight, Dean and Timmy tell her that they rode it through the Valley between formations to complete

OPPOSITE: The "fastest safest descent," East Ledges of El Cap (photo by Steph Davis)

Dean and Beth on the tandem bike in Yosemite (photo by Steph Davis)

their triple linkup climb, and then simply pedaled over to come fetch us. Never one for an undramatic finish, Beth cruises over to El Cap Meadow with Dean to retrieve a car.

Before noon, we are all back at the meadow where we started only five days before, this time surrounded by piles of stinking wall gear instead of piles of clean wall gear. Russ and I gingerly begin sorting through the heap while people swarm around Beth to congratulate her. Unbeknownst to us, the whole community of Yosemite locals has been watching her on El Cap, cheering her on. Dean tells us that the ladies who work at the deli have been asking him every day "how that little paraplegic girl is doing up on El Cap."

Industrious gear shuffling gives way to lounging in the meadow.

Beth and I gaze up at the Zodiac together, now with the eyes of climbers who've just been there.

"You know, Steph," Beth says eventually, "I don't feel like that climb was about me being paralyzed or doing it in a special way. It was about just being on El Cap with friends and all of us helping each other."

"I know," I say.

"And I can't stop thinking about how there's no way we could have done it without each person's abilities. If you and Russ weren't such good wall climbers, and if Dean and Timmy weren't so strong and fast and funny, there's no way this all could have happened."

"Well, and if you couldn't do four thousand pull-ups," I point out.

"But if Kevin and Barry hadn't sewn my burrito, and if my brother hadn't gotten me my ATV so I could practice jumaring on the ski-lift tower, and if Christian hadn't driven out to Yosemite with me. . . . "

I smile thinking of the energy that so many people poured into this single goal. Looking up at El Cap, I see something even bigger and stronger than the smooth sea of granite.

Tahir Tower in the Kondus Valley, Pakistan (photo by Steph Davis)

6

RUNNING AROUND

This mirror inside me shows . . .
I can't say what, but I can't not know.
I run from body. I run from spirit.
I do not belong anywhere.
—Rumi

I WONDER SOMETIMES WHY climbers embrace climbing so ecstatically, with a passion that feels spiritual, even religious. For years, I never questioned this deep love. I simply realized that I had been looking for something for a long time and had somehow miraculously found it before I even knew it was missing. Now, when I consider the mainstream Western culture that produced me, I see there is something seriously missing for a lot of people. An altered experience of reality is fundamental to a spiritual worldview. Perhaps that is what climbers glimpse—sometimes in the mountains, sometimes when reaching deep within to push past physical limits. Many of us have never felt it before, and we will give anything to get closer to it in the only way we know how.

I often hear people call climbing a selfish, egocentric pursuit. I consider this idea a lot. On the surface, as a sport or activity, this may be true. But for most soul climbers, climbing has never been merely about athletics. Climbing has shown me how to look beyond myself and my own desires. It has taught me how to be a part of a community, rather than living in a narrow world of my own making. I have learned, painfully, how to accept help from others. I have learned that my powerful emotions can be my greatest strength, as well as my greatest weakness. Physically and intellectually, climbing has tugged me into the larger world, beyond my own culture and comfort zone. Above all, climbing has shown me the existence of forces beyond the seen world. It has taught me to ponder the meaning of reality. It has shown me that I am small.

OUT OF BOUNDS

It's Islamabad hot. A ceiling fan spins lethargically in the dim, desk-crowded room in northern Pakistan. The Ministry of Tourism is dingy and intimidating.

Sunk in jet lag, Dave, Brady, Jimmy, and I balance tiny saucers and cups of hot sugared tea on our knees. Jimmy and Brady, friends since childhood in Minnesota, glance at each other as the minister of tourism gives us the runaround. Apart from Dave, who doesn't talk much anyway, our silence betrays our nervousness. I imagine that to the minister the four of us must look pretty similar—just more sweaty, long-haired American climbers clutching wrinkled documents.

Jimmy is the expedition leader, since this whole Kondus trip was his idea. He's the only one really paying attention when the minister drops the bomb.

While the government of Pakistan will gladly issue a permit for our climb, "the military is under no obligation to honor it," he says, as casually as he has offered to refill our tea.

Because of its proximity to the Siachen Glacier in Kashmir, the Kondus Valley where we want to go has been closed to foreigners and under military control for twenty years. Since 1947, both Pakistan and India have claimed Kashmir and have fought three full-scale wars over the region.

The fighting began just after World War II, when Britain let go of India and split the subcontinent into two countries. The Muslim majority became Pakistan in the west, and the Hindus formed India to the south and east, an emotional, faith-driven split. The wild terrain of Kashmir has been a constant bone of contention, sitting on the border of the two countries.

To make the situation more volatile, the Muslim majority in Kashmir was ruled by a Hindu, Raja Hari Singh, who gave Kashmir to India when Pakistan invaded at the time of partition. The Muslims were outraged, and hostilities have torn the region ever since. Neither side will budge. Now that both countries are nuclear powers, Kashmir could trigger a holocaust. The four of us just want to stay out of trouble—and get into the mysterious Kondus Valley to investigate tales of unclimbed peaks and towers.

The minister stamps and signs the permit and hands it to Jimmy. "Good luck," he says sincerely. My heart sinks. We'd been so worried about trying to get this government permit that we hadn't even considered that in a military zone the military outranks the government. Any underling army official in the Kondus could take one look at our permit and laugh us back to the States.

I look into my teacup, thinking of the thousands of dollars and miles we have burned through to get here. We all agreed that this trip was a risk—going to some random valley in Pakistan with no photos, no maps, no information. We braced ourselves to find anything from granite walls to alpine peaks to choss piles. Now it looks like we might not even get to see the place.

Our depressing visit to the Ministry of Tourism transforms Team Kondus into Team Hotel Room. We glower at the haulbags and steal a copy of *Shogun* back and forth from each other. Fortunately Jimmy has the unique ability to get anyone to do almost anything (evidence: four climbers in a hotel room in Islamabad, trying to go to some random valley near a war zone). Before I can finish a chapter of *Shogun,* he has somehow wangled his way into a private parade car with Nazir Sabir, the country's newest hero and the first Pakistani to summit Everest. Then he is off meeting Shah Jahan, a Pakistan International Airlines official and a friend of Nazir's, who also has lots of friends. Brigadier General Muhammed Tahir controls the Kondus Valley and the Dansum military base inside it. In no time, we are all bouncing in the back of a Land Cruiser toward General Tahir's headquarters in the remote outpost of Khapalu.

We are escorted through a garden into a room with sofas and armchairs. Servants circle in and out, supplying us with snacks, coffee, and tea.

Over six feet tall, the imposing general speaks perfect military-academy English and has smile lines around his eyes. He looks relaxed and Western in a polo shirt and jeans. By a preposterous coincidence, Tahir was a liaison officer years ago on Reinhold Messner's Karakorum expeditions, and he sees no reason at all why climbers shouldn't go into the Kondus.

"There is one beautiful tower in the Kondus," the general says after we are all seated with the requisite teacups on our knees. "But I think it may be impossible to climb. There are many other things too. Just give me a tinkle when you have set your ledge on the wall so I can come see you climbing."

We lapse into a stunned silence as he whips out a map marked SECRET and starts showing us which military checkpoints we'll pass through and which areas have big granite towers.

"I will send an officer with you to clear up any troubles you might have traveling through the checkpoints. But don't worry. He will camp with the military and leave once you are safely in the Kondus," he says expansively. "I know how mountaineers are. You don't want him to interfere with your climbs. When you are there in the Kondus, don't worry about permits or the military. Do as you like."

Dazed, we climb back into the jeep with a personal letter of permission from the general. Better still, he sends a Lieutenant Johar to personally escort us through the checkpoints.

———————————+———————————

We're cocky at the first checkpoint, a metal gate with a uniformed guard, and we take turns posing for photos under the "Foreigners Are Prohibited" sign. The village leader takes one look at our permit and letter and tells Zahid, our cook, to forget it. "Can't you read the sign?" he says in Balti.

Undaunted by the local politicking, Lieutenant Johar steps forward, says something snooty in Urdu, and within minutes we're back in the jeep going in the right direction.

"What happened, Zahid?"

"Much strong speaking," Johar answers with a laugh. "I say to village man, Brigadier General Tahir gives special permission to these people. If you are a bigger man than the brigadier general, write this in a letter. We will go and take it to him."

Johar grins at us, and Jimmy christens him Johar Superstar. We're all chuckling when the jeep swerves, hits a chicken that had wandered onto the road, and jolts to a stop. A villager with a knife sprints toward us. I can sense Brady preparing to do something Viking-like if necessary as a circle of villagers closes in on us. With no warning, our driver leaps out, grabs the knife, and frantically beheads the crushed chicken. The villagers turn away, annoyed. I look at Dave, baffled. He shrugs.

"I think the chicken was already dead," Brady says.

Jimmy nods. "Muslim code. You can't eat roadkill."

Johar Superstar strong-speaks us through checkpoints all day, and we finally turn into the promised valley. The first thing we see is General Tahir's tower, starkly silhouetted against a snowy mountain backdrop. The second thing we see is the dirt road that winds all the way to its base. I'm overwhelmed. Unclimbed seven-thousand-meter peaks and rock spires litter both sides of the valley. And there are several high narrow valleys shooting away from this main one.

The road is an unexpected bonus, but scouting by jeep is mostly a tease. Brady and I hike up a side valley and find a lifetime's worth of climbing on rock, snow, and ice. But I keep looking back at the main valley, at Tahir's tower. From our high vantage point in this valley, the tower presents a sweep of pale, sheer-shaven gray granite as clean and appealing as the Nose of El Capitan. To skip it would be like Yosemite climbing legend Warren Harding leaving a car full of gear at the base of El Cap and schlepping loads miles into Tenaya Canyon in hopes of finding another good rock to climb.

"What do you think?" I ask, squinting through a spotting scope at the tower. "Two thousand feet?"

"It's hard to tell. It has to be foreshortened," Brady says.

A single dihedral system runs from bottom to top, right up the middle of the tower. The first half looks slabby and dirty, but the upper half looks like immaculate granite. Overall the line is one of the most continuous corner systems I've ever seen, and it's impossible to pass up. But the hundred-degree heat at our eleven-thousand-foot elevation is hard to take, especially after two weeks of roasting in the city. We glance yearningly at the snow in the higher valleys, then set up base camp in the dusty flat zone below the tower.

The jeep driver takes us to a river crossing where we fill our blue expedition barrels with water. Zahid looks unenthusiastic about the site but dutifully sets up the cook tent. A scorching rock climb on a tower isn't exactly what any of us was expecting, but hopefully we can quickly climb it and then move up to a cooler place.

Our base camp is a petri dish for bacteria. Dave and Jimmy are hit hard by the infamous Pakistani crud and have fevers of 104 degrees. Brady and I decide to start climbing, intending to fix lines to an obvious ledge partway up the tower. When Jimmy and Dave recover, we can all jug up the fixed lines together and cruise to the top.

———————+———————

The climbing starts off dirty and crumbly. It's insanely hot. Brady and I sweat and grovel, knocking down continuous showers of dirt, gravel, and thornbushes. At the end of the day we've fixed a thousand feet of rope, and we haven't even reached the ledge we thought was eight hundred feet up the wall. Feeling foolish at having so underestimated the tower's size, we rap to give Dave and Jimmy the news. The tower is bigger than El Cap and hotter than the Salathe Wall in high summer. So far the climbing has been spectacularly bad, but after two weeks of hotel rooms and kidney-jolting jeep rides, any climbing is good climbing.

Dave passes off his fever to me and gets to recuperate by jugging a thousand feet of fixed line. The next pitch is a crumbling 5.10 slab pitch. Dave pads up fifty feet of tenuous balancey moves and disintegrating footholds until he can hand-drill a quarter-inch bolt. Forty feet above the bolt, he sets his next piece, a pecker—one of the smallest pins you can place. Jimmy frantically beefs up his belay anchor, pounding in pin after pin as Dave's crumbling footholds rain down on him. Dave finishes the pitch with no comment until the next day when he stoically remarks, "Well. You only get a few pitches like that in your life."

Three days of climbing have taken us fifteen hundred feet up the wall, and we can see that we're not even halfway. For another week we are rendered nearly helpless by bouts of fever and nausea. Whenever we are able to stand, we haul hundreds of pounds of water up the wall. Somehow Brady avoids the sickness, seemingly through sheer stubbornness. Bags full of crampons, down jackets, and shell clothing sit uselessly in base camp.

Village girl and her chicken, Kondus Valley (photo by Steph Davis)

In the week it takes to fix and haul we are besieged by village men. They stay in our camp for hours, looking through the scope and at us. After days of intense scrutiny I learn my first words of Balti from Zahid. "*Chee soong? Chee lahl teht??!!*" What's the problem? What are you looking at??!!

"These people want to know if you will find firewood on this tower," Zahid says. "No one has ever climbed it to look for wood. Also, they ask if you will look for mountain oil."

"Mountain oil?"

"Yes. Good for old men to eat for . . . strength. It is black like tar, always in mountains and rocks. You see it?"

Mountain oil??

———|———

The local women pass by our base camp every day on their never-ending search for firewood. They are amazed to see me living in my own tent, apparently no one's wife. They also don't believe I'm really one of the climbers. To prove it, I put on rock shoes and let them dip into my chalkbag. Thrilled, they form a fan club of sorts and chant "Stuff! Stuff!" each time they pass by.

The women start to pay me "special visits," crowding around my tent and into the vestibule. I show them photos of my dog and boyfriend. They bring me a chicken to admire. They are fascinated by my French braids, showing me that they only know how to weave the regular kind in their long black hair. When they see my scratched bare arms, they gesture that I should climb in the long, pajama-like *shalwar kameez* and shawl to protect my skin.

"Ladies say special prayers for you," Zahid tells me. "They pray for you to have success on your climb and also have a son."

"No!" I yelp. "Just success!"

It turns out that praying for a son is the kindest sentiment a Pakistani woman can wish upon another. In Pakistan, women are considered commodities to be sold, or even killed for any act—real or imagined—that dishonors the family, such as attempting to divorce an abusive husband. Even more horrifically, a woman can be murdered as punishment for the perceived crime of being raped. In Pakistan, a woman can be killed if her husband simply dreams of his wife committing adultery. Every year, hundreds if not thousands of women suffer such "honor killings," most of which go unreported.

"Tell them to pray for me to have a daughter," I tell Zahid firmly.

He laughs uncertainly, but I insist. The women look shocked, then start giggling.

"Ladies ask why you don't like men," Zahid says.

I start laughing too.

Jimmy, Brady, and Dave stay busy giving National Outdoor Leadership School–type how-to seminars to Captain Abdullah, a tall young officer from Dansum. He and his special-forces men use climbing skills to cross the glaciers and climb to the high posts. They are fascinated by our high-tech gear.

"These are very nice, much better than our equipment," Abdullah says, admiring the piton rack. None of us has the heart to tell him that the pins are our most archaic gear.

Soon Captain Abdullah wants to know if he can join us on the climb. A little flustered, Brady explains that we only have enough portaledge space for four.

"Then will you bolt this Pakistani flag to the tower?"

"Uh, sure."

"And is it possible to spray-paint General Tahir's name on the mountain?"

After several more days of toiling on the slabs, the four of us are relatively healthy, and we have moved all sorts of gear and water to our high point on the wall, about a thousand feet up. So far we've been able to free every pitch, mostly because the rock is too crumbly to aid, and the prospect for more free climbing looks good. Overhead, the perfect dihedral launches up like a massive laundry chute. The granite is gray and clean, and the corner crack runs above us endlessly, starting as a podded seam that widens into an off-width crack and then a chimney over hundreds of feet. Far beyond the corner system, a roof blocks our view.

Pitch after pitch, we layback, stem, jam, and chimney this corner that seems as ceaseless as Pakistan's war with India. Soon I've forgotten how to climb anything but a right-facing dihedral.

When we finally reach the roof, it's Jimmy's lead. It starts with an intimidating curtain of hollow rock. We anxiously await the report from Jimmy about the hidden rock above as he disappears from sight.

"It's the dream corner!" he yells from above. "It's awesome!"

Thin immaculate aid corners stretch above, for who knows how long.

Our second ledge camp, above pitch twenty-one, rewards us with views of the distant peaks and valleys. On a steep scree slope across from us, yaklike dzo graze peacefully near two herders. All day, black dots drift around the slopes. At night we see the lights of the herders' fires.

"I wonder what they think of our portaledges and our headlamps at night," Brady muses. Despite a supposed cease-fire, constant distant shelling reminds us of the region's ongoing violence and adds to the mélange of realities.

I look out at the desolate, sparsely populated valleys and think again of how preposterous the fighting seems. According to Captain Abdullah, the conflict is a problem of religion and pride.

"Neither side will ever win this war," he told me. "There are far more casualties from altitude sickness and the elements than from fighting. Some of the posts are at twenty-two thousand feet, and soldiers must man them throughout the winter. The conditions for both Indians and Pakistanis are very harsh. But neither will leave. The people who live here have always been Pakistani. We will never give this region up. Our faith allows us to endure the terrible conditions."

On pitch twenty-two I tap a pecker gently into a seam. Four hundred feet below, a Pakistani flag flutters beneath the portaledge, as promised. Dave and Jimmy chat by radio to General Tahir, who has driven a jeep here just to see us on the wall.

"We are calling this Tahir Tower," Jimmy tells him.

Far below, soldiers and villagers cluster around our tents.

"I am extremely honored!" the general radios back.

Later, we ask Zahid what the local people call the tower.

Pakistani men scoping the Americans on Tahir Tower (photo by Steph Davis)

"Local name means 'Blood Coming Down Tower,'" Zahid says. "But they very happy with Tahir name, honoring brigadier general. This is very important!"

The spectacular aid corner abruptly dead-ends at a blocky headwall we had spied through the scope. It is overhanging drastically, and the only climbable features are fractured blocks that are chossy even by American Fork Canyon standards.

Jimmy, however, is up for the challenge. Which is good because it's his lead. I settle into the swing seat for a long aid belay and start racking the screamers, special slings that will tear out under a fall to absorb shock instead of putting all the fall force directly on a bad aid placement. It looks like he'll need them.

I haven't seen Jimmy climb hard aid before, and I'm relieved to see how cautiously he moves in his aiders, easing onto upside-down toucans and knifeblades wedged behind the questionable blocks. I sing Santana songs and privately calculate how close he'll get to the sloping ledge below my belay if everything rips out.

"How's it looking, Jimmy?"

"Fine! I just don't want to drill."

Several hours go by, then Jimmy crests the headwall and we're back in dihedral land. We still can't see the top.

Dave and Brady continue up the corners the next day, and Jimmy and I jug their lines wondering just how far the summit really is. We've been climbing for over a week and must be three thousand feet up. We feel like we're close to the top, but there's no end in sight.

My next pitch looks like a splitter crack. Happy for a break from aid climbing, I dig out my rock shoes and eagerly throw cams onto a shoulder sling. Maybe we won't be up here forever after all, I think, wedging hands and feet into the crack. But in seconds, I'm grabbing gear, gingerly dividing my weight between crumbling cam placements and expanding jams. Drat.

On the next pitch, Jimmy's body weight rips a textbook #2 Camalot out of the disintegrating rock. Though he flips upside-down and slams face-first into a small ledge, he refuses to back down from the pitch. I don't get a good look at him until I reach his anchor on a ledge covered with stinking black droppings (mountain oil?). Jimmy smiles through a crust of blood.

"I think I'm all right," he slurs alarmingly.

"Jimmy, you're going down right now," I order, pointing to the fixed lines that lead down to the portaledges.

Back at the ledges, Dave and Brady tape Jimmy's face back together and jug up the lines to continue climbing. They top out of the dihedrals, at last, and find a ridge leading to a slender Canyonlands-style spire.

Tahir summit dance (photo by Jimmy Chin)

The bizarre summit pillar is a spectacular finale. The four of us go together, to summit as a team. Dave zips up an exposed slab to a table-size ledge. Clouds and drizzle roll in, and the last pitch looks thin and crumbly. I high-step in aiders between surprisingly solid peckers and toucans until I can break free and slab around a narrow arête to the summit.

Surrounded by my three friends and the mist-filled valleys and peaks of the Kondus, I feel unbelievably lucky. I think of the events that led to this instant, as fragile and improbable as the choss band we climbed through.

———————|———————

We rappel for two days, conscientiously tossing down choice sticks of firewood from the lower pitches. Villagers stand around the base gathering up the twigs. Zahid and his younger brother Ali are waiting with huge smiles to grab haulbags and hustle us down to base camp for a celebratory dinner. Zahid has outdone himself preparing nori rolls, a specialty he has learned from Japanese clients. Captain Abdullah arrives and disdainfully eyes the rolls we are devouring.

"If you are finished climbing, come visit Dansum," he says. "We will have a real celebration feast."

Only Zahid and I hesitate to accept the invitation. General Tahir's one warning had been to stay clear of Dansum, and Zahid has been on the verge of an ulcer all month from being around so many military officers.

"Nine months ago, no more smoking," he tells me miserably. "Here in pucking Kondus, I much smoking."

I also worry that the soldiers might harass me. Zahid and I reluctantly agree to go with everyone to the base but to bail if it's weird.

As we drive toward the cement walls of Dansum, my imagination goes wild. Could this be an elaborate plot to get better climbing gear? What if they throw us in bamboo cages and make us play Russian roulette?

Inside the compound, Captain Abdullah and Major Safdar, another well-mannered young officer, solemnly usher us into a barracks. Jimmy, Brady, Dave, and I sit silently as Abdullah rummages through some piles. Top-secret military plans? Grisly battle souvenirs? No one breathes. At

Dave and Jimmy in Pakistani military parkas, Dansum Military Base (photo by Steph Davis)

last, Abdullah turns with an armful of photo albums brimming with snapshots of his family and army buddies.

Things do get more exciting when we go outside and Abdullah hands me an AK-47 and asks if I'd like to fire it. It doesn't look like much of a gun to me. It's not even all that heavy. Still, I grip it nervously and brace it against my shoulder.

Cringing, I fire an ear-splitting shot into the air, followed by dead silence until I burst into relieved laughter. Captain Abdullah hands the gun back to an expressionless soldier. I can't stop giggling as we walk among the barracks, hardly noticing for once the eyes that follow me. Still, Abdullah feels courtesy-bound to apologize for the stares.

"I think these men have never seen a woman fire an AK-47 before," he says.

I look at the line of unwavering stares. "I think these men have never seen a woman before."

After target practice we check out the Pakistanis' climbing equipment: puffy white down suits and flimsy crampons that you can bend with bare hands. Abdullah and Safdar sneak off and come back with commemorative plaques for us. I read mine, touched. "Siachen Glacier, 2000." I guess they must keep them handy for times like this. Abdullah takes lots of pictures for his photo album.

When dinner arrives at last, I am shocked by the scale of it. A huge number of chickens have been slaughtered for this occasion: chicken curry, chicken with potatoes, barbecued chicken, fried chicken, stewed chicken, chicken and lentils, chicken with rice. I wonder if there are any chickens left alive in Dansum. We eat like we've been on a wall for two weeks, and then kick back with after-dinner Pepsis (Muslim code—no alcohol).

Although Major Safdar is technically Adbullah's superior officer, the two are mainly close pals in this isolated outpost.

"You can never understand our culture," Safdar says, and to prove it points at the army doctor who hasn't said a word all evening.

"His fiancée's parents killed her for becoming engaged to him."

I am horrified.

"Oh, he's all right now. His family found another wife and now he has children." The doctor nods complacently.

"I'm a bachelor," Captain Abdullah remarks.

We drive off the next morning, waving goodbye to the armed guard at the gate. General Tahir is waiting for us at Khapalu and is delighted and relieved to see us. He insists that we stay for yet another celebration dinner and soon has us all laughing and calling him Terry, just like Reinhold Messner had done. We promise to stay in touch and to send photos of Tahir Tower.

HOUSE OF WIND

Patagonia. The wind is thundering above. From the shelter of the langa trees I hear it whirling and leaping out on the glacier. There's no hope of good weather tomorrow. We could just as well stay at base camp.

"Stay," say the Italians, "tonight we make pizza!"

"Stay," say the French, "tonight we are making fondue!"

But if I prowl around Campo Bridwell for one more day, I may kill someone. Maybe Dean. Better to forge across the glacier in a headwind and arrive soaked and exhausted at high camp so we can sit in a smaller tent, eat less interesting food, and feel productive as we accomplish nothing.

We slide down almost vertical scree and baked dirt to the moraine. Pack straps and pigtails whip my face as we wind up and around crevasses. It's been almost an hour since we left Bridwell.

The wind races about maniacally as we crest the final rise. I step

Dean and gentle wind, Patagonia (photo by Steph Davis)

cramponless onto bare ice, and a two-directional gust hurls me down, then spins away faster than I can refill my lungs.

Shakily, I rise. Dean and I look at each other wide-eyed and dart for the nearest flat spot in the ice, dropping to our knees just as the wind rushes in again. It pummels us thoroughly and then spirals off, allowing us to scuttle a little farther before it wheels back and dives in harder.

Caught, I freeze like a deer in headlights and drive my ski poles down, bracing desperately until I can flatten. Again, the wind twists away. Again, I bolt across uneven ice in its ebb until I hear the whir of approaching jet engines and, gun-shy, fling myself down.

But this time the wind leaps high without touching us, leaving me to stagger up foolishly from under my pack. And then, capriciously and with an impressive backhand, it pivots and slams me flat.

Forward progress has lost its meaning. It is simply a thing I do. There is no end. There is no goal. There is only dogged, fitful motion. The wind consumes all time and speech, breathes them in and out like harmonica chords.

I think of pilgrims prostrating themselves with each step toward Mecca. A truly incomprehensible form of worship, I've always thought . . . and yet, here I am.

7

KNOCKING FROM THE INSIDE

I have lived on the lip
of insanity, wanting to know reasons,
knocking on a door. It opens.
I've been knocking from the inside!
—Rumi

I ONCE MET A NATURALIST in a Wyoming bar who had spent months in Joshua Tree studying desert tortoises. I was thrilled and fascinated. I had never seen a tortoise in Joshua Tree, just lots of granite climbs and Dr. Seuss–like trees. I interrogated him mercilessly about the creatures' habits, until finally the poor guy agreed to send me a copy of his research paper (which he actually did, some weeks later).

What astonished me most was that these tortoises don't urinate for months and months. Instead, they internally reprocess their moisture over and over, until finally they excrete a nasty, dark substance that has been completely stripped of any useable moisture. People who are shipwrecked have been driven to drink their own urine in order to survive. The result is somewhat the same, but for humans the process is hideously unpleasant, inefficient, and not very healthy. For tortoises, it's no big deal. They don't even have to drink.

To me, this is yet another reminder of how much better adapted animals are, when it comes right down to it. They survive quite happily in environments that are death zones for humans. This seems ironic, because in school I was told that humans are superior to other animals because we can adapt the natural world to ourselves. But as time goes

OPPOSITE: Talking with Fletch in Hueco Tanks, Texas (photo by Kennan Harvey)

by, I'm starting to think this is our biggest weakness. For me, a funda-mental lesson of climbing is that survival is about adapting oneself to the natural world. I have come to see that I am a natural creature too, and I am not in charge. The smartest thing I can do is figure out how to cooperate and try not to cause too much trouble.

With no prior planning, I surprised myself five years ago by spon-taneously becoming vegan. I wish I had known before what I know now, which is that many world-class athletes are vegan. I always bought into the myth that climbers and alpinists need animal protein to be strong. Instead, I have found out that my body works better and stays healthier without it. And over time I have become even more certain that all life is sacred. No one deserves to be mistreated or killed, and I think that in many ways animals are smarter and better than humans. Certainly, I aspire to be as good as my dog Fletcher. She has been my greatest friend and role model in life.

I have read accounts of Native Americans hunting for their own meat and feeling the animal's power entering their spirit. Since becom-ing vegan, I have felt something similar, though perhaps the opposite. In certain moments, alone in wild places or pushing myself to the edge on a climb, I suddenly feel a surge of power that feels like it's coming from the energy of all the lives I haven't taken. I know that sounds weird. But I am not making it up.

WE'VE ALWAYS RUN

I skirt around a jeep laboring up the slickrock and dodge two mountain bikers grinding their lowest gears. In the twenty-first century, going low-tech is almost an eccentricity, but I still think running is the best way to cover rough terrain. All I'm carrying is a pair of shoes on my feet and a windbreaker around my waist. Being a dog, Fletcher doesn't have to carry anything. We grin at each other in complicity, and Fletcher careens out into the desert after a rabbit, ears plastered back for speed. Show off. Just because she has four legs.

I'm tranced out, lulled by the motion of my feet on dirt and rock, the rhythmic beat of my arms, the cadence of Fletch's hind legs. Lizards dart away from my footsteps like water splashing. What legged creature does not run? There are a few things the human body has always done, I think, and running must be one of them.

I'm flat out happy in the desert sun, feeling the purity of doing what I'm built for. Fletcher is feeling exactly the same. She radiates tangible doggy joy. Why do I always think I'm training when I run? That's not it at all. I'm simply easing into my natural state.

TRAVELING LIGHT

Yosemite Valley, long summer days. It's really too hot to climb, but I can't leave this place. I range like a coyote, looking, smelling, casing my domain. Daylight wires me like a drug. There will be all winter to rest.

I cruise from one end of the Valley to the other, sometimes in light, sometimes in dark, scouting from all points. Hiding from the sun, I climb alone and carry almost nothing, traveling three-dimensionally on earth and rock. For days at a time, I take the same routes, watching for little changes, sniffing the wind.

Most climbers have gone to cooler places. But I find some signs. A new chalk mark high up on Half Dome, fresh shoe prints in the forest above El Cap. I'm too wild to talk to people, too shy. I just want to know where they've been. The ravens seem to recognize me.

I can't rest. I hardly sleep. My body is permanently sore. Ragged hair, dirty feet, little cuts that don't heal. Some days I eat frantically, others I go hungry. The solstice is near. I feel subtle differences in air temperature each morning, changes of moisture snaking in and out. Soon days will grow shorter. Winter will come. I have to keep moving.

ETERNAL SUNRISE

December nights lengthen in the Utah desert. I crawl into the back of my truck and wrap myself around Fletcher in the coldest part of night. Soon I'm sleeping more than I'm awake. The world is groggy, dream-like. I need more sun. It's time to head south, to Texas.

In Hueco Tanks, December has more light. I can climb in shorts. But my mind wanders throughout these carefree days of desert bouldering.

Pink Flamingo, Indian Creek, Utah (photo by Eric Perlman)

This living is too easy. At night I vigilantly file torn skin off my fingertips and mentally rehearse the moves of sequential boulder problems. But I'm thinking of snow and ice and granite, of carrying a dense pack up a glacier for timeless hours. I can almost feel the weight of leather boots and crampons on my feet, ski poles in my gloved hands. The wind is calling. It's time to head still farther south, to Patagonia.

January is high summer in Argentine Patagonia, but only the long hours of daylight show it. The mountains are wintry and frigid, in maelstroms of clouds. My Argentine friends seem to grow more beautiful and vivacious every year, and the wind seems to grow stronger. Dean and I are all fierce energy, racehorses at the gate. This season we will work harder than ever before. The weather will not keep us off the mountains. We carry gear and strategize, dig endless snow caves. Even in storms, we climb and we retreat.

By March, this stolen second summer is fading. Days grow shorter, nights colder. I feel tired and worn out. My clothing is smelly and patched, my crampons have shrunk from too much sharpening. I've been wet for months. In the embryonic dimness of the snow cave, my dank sleeping bag is filled with clammy glove liners and socks. I lie dreaming of Fletcher's warm fur. I yearn to climb rock bare-handed, carrying only a rack and a chalkbag, to wake up in my dry truck, to drink coffee without clumps of powdered soy milk. I long to wear cotton underwear and change them every day, to see my bare legs again.

Life has gotten too hard here. The wind forces a flood of snow into the cave entrance. I open my eyes and look up at drops of condensation clustered above my face. At home, in the desert, spring is coming. Even here in the snow cave, I can feel it. It's time to move again, time to follow the sun.

8

BEGINNER'S MIND

Undoubtedly, the mind is restless and hard to control. But it can be trained by constant practice and by freedom from desire.
—B. K. S. Iyengar

CLIMBING IS REALLY GREAT, we all love climbing. But what's interesting to me is what happens in my head or in my life because of it. Ultimately, I think climbing is a vehicle for exploration—of the world, of the self.

When I first started climbing, all that mattered to me was passion. Everything else seemed superficial or impure, sullied by material concerns. I see now that there are many ways to enter the nonmaterial realm. Climbing just happens to be the path I use. I have also learned that spirituality does not mean simply rejecting the physical world. Rather, it demands balance and harmony on the material level. As time goes by, I have learned to embrace the analytical and pragmatic aspects of my personality. I realize that these are strengths, not character flaws. Being anal-retentive is actually a good quality for a climber.

Big climbing projects have become an important outlet for my self-expression as a climber, demanding equal parts emotion and intellectualism. I love the cycle of hard work and scrupulous planning, capped by all-out passionate effort. The balancing act confuses me, though. On a hard climb, if I don't give everything I have, I can't succeed. Yet, if I want it too much, I crack under the pressure and can't allow myself to surrender to an effortless state.

OPPOSITE: On the one-day ascent of Free Rider, El Cap (photo by Heinz Zak)

ABOUT TIME

My watch is a curious object. The alarm beeps in the dark and I go to make coffee. Or it beeps in the dark and I've just returned to my sleeping bag after twenty hours of motion. Or it beeps as I'm an hour into crunching up snowfields, or it beeps when I'm cooking dinner. It's seemingly random. There is no order. I need it, though, the watch, because sometimes I want to know what date I'm supposed to be in.

"Time! Time!" the hobbit squeaked in terror, as Gollum demanded an answer to his riddle. Time was what Bilbo was begging for, and it was also the answer that saved his life. I think of him as I hike up the steep hill to the lake in the dark. My mind fastens onto the word, repeats it with each footstep. Time. Time. Time.

Three more weeks here is starting to seem like not enough time. But it is also too much. Gone are thoughts of pushing it on short rock climbs, improving daily, being on a nice, logical training schedule. Eating breakfast in the morning, going to sleep at night. What have I achieved, precisely, in almost two months in Patagonia? My culture and upbringing teach me to set goals and achieve them. Patagonia just laughs.

"Minutes pass, or are they hours?" Kurt Diemberger asks dreamily, recalling an early ascent in the Alps. What is this thing we call time? Jorge Luis Borges, the brilliant Argentine writer, spent years reflecting on the puzzle: "I do not pretend to know what sort of thing time is—or even if it is a 'thing'—but I feel that the passage of time and time itself are a single mystery and not two." And in a different, even more mystical mind frame, he wrote, "Time is a river that sweeps me along, but I am the river; it is a tiger that mangles me, but I am the tiger; it is a fire that consumes me, but I am the fire."

How can an hour be so different? I thought, was taught, that it is a unit of measurement. Dependable, like an ounce or a meter, reliable and the same, a yardstick with which to measure my world. But we all know that an hour spent with a loved one bears no resemblance to an hour spent in a stiff chair, waiting for punishment. I'm not even sure what an hour means any more. Is it the wind that has erased all that I thought I once knew?

Dean descending Fitzroy in a storm (photo by Steph Davis)

"I used to be respectable and chaste and stable, but who can stand in this strong wind and remember those things?" Rumi asks. "The same wind that uproots trees makes the grasses shine. The lordly wind loves the weakness and the lowness of grasses. Never brag of being strong. Wind destroys and wind protects. There is no reality but God, says the completely surrendered sheikh."

Here in Patagonia, I learn what Sufi mystics have known since the thirteenth century, and what others have known for even longer. "It was only the first night, but a number of centuries had already preceded it," Rafael Cansinos Assens writes cryptically. And Marcus Aurelius: "Remember that all things turn and turn again in the same orbits, and for the spectator it is the same to watch for a century or two or infinitely."

Infinity and time, like rappel ropes, have been irretrievably tangled into each other by the wind. I feel that I glimpse the snarl but can only pluck futilely at a few loops before the wind snatches the whole ball away from me again. Why am I here? What is the point of my presence? What difference would it make to anything if I were somewhere else and not hiking up and down hills in these so-called hours of my existence? I begin to wonder if I do exist. The wind sweeps my mind bare.

BREAKING FREE

My earliest memories are of piano keyboards, my legs dangling from the bench. By the time I was eighteen, I was playing six hours a day. I was excused from most of my high-school classes to hole up in a practice room. Working out hard sections alone was fun and engaging. Sight-reading, with no expectations, just the intensity of the moment, was exhilarating. But performing pieces that I had rehearsed minutely was unbelievably stressful. In the ruthless world of classical music, failure to perform perfectly is unimaginable, sheer humiliation. But this had been my life since I was three, and I never questioned it.

The first day I went climbing, as a college freshman, I quit music cold turkey. Looking back over fourteen years of climbing, I see that what I ran to wasn't really so different. For years I shied away from working routes and then redpointing them—making a clean ascent without falling, having studied and worked out the route section by section. Just like performing a long-rehearsed piece of music, these kinds of projects were so stressful, and I worried about blowing all the hard work and ruining everything. Music had trained me to work my weaknesses, so I forced myself to do the same thing with routes occasionally, but I hated the pressure I felt. I preferred to onsight climbs, pushing myself to perfection on a first try, or to have adventures in the mountains. When the stakes approached life and death, I always rose to the occasion, swept away by the intensity of the moment, just as I had always managed to scrape through when sight-reading a new piece of music. As a climber, I found that the risk of physical damage actually scared me less than the artificial pressure of simple failure on a sport route. Although I had tried to take a completely different direction in life, I was indelibly stamped by my formative years at the piano.

Before I even knew what a big wall was, the desire to climb long routes naturally pulled me to Yosemite Valley. Like every climber who comes to the Valley, I soon discovered that it truly has everything—bouldering, cragging, easy free solos, long free climbs, aid routes, backcountry adventures. But with each visit, I found the Valley a more impossible place. I loved the climbing, but I was easily overwhelmed by the crowds and nonsensical rules. I couldn't deal with fast-food stands, tourists who stopped in the middle of the road to gawk at a squirrel, and most of all the endless talk about climbing. I didn't want to talk about climbing or other climbers, I just wanted to do it. I felt like a rat in a cage in Camp 4, and was always sleeping in the forest and getting harassed by rangers essentially for existing. Being a dog, my beloved companion Fletcher was even more guilty of existing and felt even more hunted than I did. I usually only lasted a few weeks in Yosemite before fleeing to the peace and normalcy of a place like Indian Creek, near Moab, or Pakistan. Yet I was always drawn back, and after marrying Dean, a devout Valley climber, I understood that I needed to make Yosemite as much my home as Moab.

From the Valley locals I learned to cruise the solo routes and to maneuver the obstacles of the Yosemite lifestyle, and from Dean I learned to escape the artificial amusement-park chaos by staying on the big walls and in the backcountry. Fletcher, the social one in the family, made plenty of friends of her own and enthusiastically joined the crew of Yosemite "derelicts" when we were up on the walls. Half Dome, Mount Watkins, and El Capitan became my second, third, and fourth homes. Gradually I learned how to live a simple, natural life in the Valley, and with it I gained the freedom to just climb. Finally I was able to experience Yosemite as a true paradise. And I soon realized that during my years of visits I had climbed most of the classic routes—it was time to start taking on bigger goals.

In early fall, I started working on Free Rider, but in a pretty aimless way. Normally when I get inspired by a route, I work relentlessly until I do it. But the idea of freeing El Cap seemed overwhelming, so I cultivated a Zen-like attitude, not truly setting it as a goal, to avoid feeling pressured. Mostly I just wanted to check it out. Using what I had learned from the other El Cap free climbers and from my habits of soloing, I bivied alone on top, rapping in to see the most difficult upper pitches.

What I quickly realized was that none of Free Rider was easy. For one thing, it has some stout off-width pitches—those awful cracks that are too big to jam and too small to crawl inside. I'd always thought I was a pretty good off-width climber, even climbing them on purpose instead of avoiding them at all costs. But on my first effort I flailed to the point of tears on the upper "easy" off-width. And the crux of the route, the Huber Pitch, stumped me completely. I had watched Dean climb it, but I couldn't reach the holds he had used. I tried different moves over and over, but no matter what tenuous position I got into I was always inches away from even touching the last face hold. I felt extremely discouraged by the reachy nature of the pitch but tried to look on the bright side—comparatively, the upper dihedral pitch often considered the redpoint crux of the route, was relatively easy for me.

By October I decided to go for the route and worry about the Huber Pitch when I got there. Free Rider is almost the same as the Salathe, varying only by three pitches at the top, and the constant traffic of big-wall climbers on the Salathe ensures that fixed lines are always in place up to Heart Ledge and often even to the top of the Hollow Flake. Typically, aid parties climb the lower twelve to fourteen pitches, descend the fixed lines, and make a big hauling day. Then they jug up the ropes to launch onto the wall. Since I didn't have a specific partner, I was able to take advantage of other parties' fixed lines to free the lower portion of the route by begging different friends to accompany me first for the Free Blast portion, and then to free the pitches to the top of the Hollow Flake. We could just rap back down at the end of the day. I am perhaps excessively independent and generally reclusive, and I hated having to ask people for help, but I could see that this was yet another opportunity to work on a weakness. Free Rider was stretching me in ways I had never anticipated.

After freeing the lower pitches, I recruited yet another friend to jug up and get on the wall with me. The day started inauspiciously. Sick of imposing on friends, I had actually paid two climbers to haul my bag to the Hollow Flake ledge the day before. We ascended the Heart lines in the dark to find there had been a communication problem and the bag was marooned two pitches below the ledge. One of my haulers was so faithful that he slept on Heart Ledge so he could help finish hauling when I got there at dawn! I was moved by his integrity, but my heart sank as I realized my effort was doomed before I even started. With so many pitches to climb that day, this immediate setback was sure to blow my timing. But it seemed ridiculous to give up before even starting. I went into overdrive, and I made it to the Alcove by evening. It was Halloween night, and after five months of record heat in the Valley it started snowing. I wouldn't even get a chance to try the upper crux pitches. The next day, we rappeled on wet ropes through the snow. I threw the soaking gear in my truck and left El Cap behind.

On the long drive to Moab, I realized that by trying and failing on Free Rider I had accepted it as a project. I'd been trying not to let that happen, because I'm kind of obsessive. I also realized that freeing El Cap, especially as an individual leader with no partner, would depend on a lot more than just the climbing. I would have to plan every element of the ascent to make sure that logistics didn't cause failure. Rather than feeling put off by this, it gave me confidence. I could use my strongest tools on this project—determination and strategy—not just pure tendon strength.

All winter, I thought about Free Rider, especially the moves on the Huber Pitch. To reach that final hold I concluded that I'd have to climb into a tenuous stance, my fingers clinging in opposite directions on a wrinkle in front of my face—as though trying to pry open an elevator door—and then explode into an all-out sideways leap to the slanting hold. If I did manage to catch it, I would need to hang on with both hands as my body flew sideways, like a cat in a hurricane latched onto a telephone pole. Two thousand feet up on El Cap. With a single spinning buttonhead for gear between me and my belayer. The move seemed completely improbable. But I realized that the body positions for setting up to leap were similar to certain yoga poses, so I did warrior poses day after day. I also realized that only two or three moves were stopping me, essentially a boulder problem. Uncharacteristically, that winter I never tied in to a rope, choosing to boulder at Big Bend and climb on my backyard wall, to increase my power for those moves. I also ran my first ultramarathon, to gain toughness for the rest of the climb. My friends in Moab wondered why I was doing all of these strange things, but I hate talking about projects before I finish them.

In March, the weather in Yosemite turned unbelievably good. I got in my truck and drove to the Valley. Analyzing the last season, I realized

Warrior pose on the summit of El Cap (photo by Heinz Zak)

that I had almost never rested. This is a bad tendency of mine—being too driven and running myself into the ground. By the time I'd gone back to Moab the previous fall, I was so worn out that I came down with the flu for a month. Climbing isn't like the piano. Without rest, there can be no improvement. I resolved to force myself to rest a lot more this season.

As usual, logistics would be the biggest problem . . . as usual, I didn't have a partner. Dean and I try not to impose on each other when it's high season in Yosemite; often we're both driven, pursuing differ-ent projects. Four days of jugging and hauling is asking a lot of anyone, and there weren't many people around this early in the year. I tried to minimize the favor by splitting up the route, because there were still fixed lines up to the Hollow Flake. Ed, a Valley local, generously gave me the first day of jugging. I freed the lower portion of the route and we rapped down together. I had officially started my attempt but was still partnerless, and it had started to rain. Dean returned from a training excursion to find me frantic with frustration, both at the weather and at having no partner lined up. "You're epic-ing," he said. "I'm going with you when it stops." I felt terrible, as he was in the middle of working on his own projects. But I was desperate. Three days later, it cleared and the forecast finally looked good.

We ascended the fixed lines to my high point and gear stash at the Hollow Flake ledge, and I switched to climbing mode, feeling rusty from all the rain days. This would be a big day, what with all the jug-ging and then having to lead the dreaded Monster off-width pitches. If all went well, at the end of the day we would be twenty-two pitches up, with the hardest off-widths behind me. At the roof crux of the first Monster off-width, the big cam I was pushing cartwheeled open and fell onto my stomach, just as I was wriggling up with my back to the ground. Terrified, I fought to stay wedged in this hideous position and get the piece back in, burning way too much energy in a fight to survive. After that, the rest of the off-widths felt simple, but I was nearly deliri-ous by the time we reached the Alcove. Still, I had to climb two more

OPPOSITE: El Capitan, from the west (photo by Jimmy Chin)

strenuous pitches, because I planned to rest on the luxurious ledge for an entire day and then jug up for the Huber Pitch before the sun hit it.

The next day at the Alcove, I ate plenty of food and did seated yoga poses. I reflected on how much work and effort I had given just to get to the crux of Free Rider. It felt like there was a lot at stake in firing the Huber Pitch. Unlike a boulder problem or a crag project, if I blew it I would be set back by a week or two and a huge amount of organizing. I couldn't ask Dean to go with me again. I'd have to start all over, scrounging for partners, doing the Free Blast, launching up the wall to the Alcove. I thought about how meticulously I had prepared and about all of the reasons why I knew I could do those moves. But I also felt a lot of doubt, because I'd never actually done them.

We woke early, packed the bag, and jugged up the lines I'd fixed the first day. The stormy weather had made it much colder than I'd been expecting. I was shaking and my feet were numb. I took off my shoes and blew into them, tried to steel myself, and started to climb. I felt strong as I climbed into the warrior stance. I tried not to wonder if the old buttonhead would hold a fall, and I jumped left as Dean gave me lots of slack. I hit the hold, but too low to keep it, feeling helpless as my hands and feet peeled off El Cap. I flew downward, banging sideways along the slab below. Dean lowered me to the belay ledge, and I untied and pulled the rope. I couldn't stop shaking.

"You're going to do it sooner or later," Dean said, "so you may as well do it now." I put on a jacket and looked up at the rock. I thought about my two most supportive friends, Craig and Laurie, and tried to focus the good energy I knew they were sending me. I started the moves again, feeling weaker but absolutely committed. When I got to the warrior stance, I leaped with everything I had. This time I latched the hold with both hands. As my body flew left, I kicked my feet against the wall and made the next long pull into the layback crack.

Still quivering, I kept my concentration until I reached the belay and then started yelping with delight. I felt stunned, like I'd just exploded through an actual wall to another place and was looking around,

OPPOSITE: Jump move on the Huber pitch (photo by Heinz Zak)

shaking off bits of drywall. When Dean reached me, I pulled my hood up and dove into the dripping, slippery Jungle Pitch, and soon we were at the Block. Things were going better than I'd hoped, and it wasn't even noon, so I decided to keep climbing. The dihedrals and the traverse would be demanding leads and could still stop me.

Scrapping up the flaring, funky jams and laybacks of the dihedral, I had the surreal feeling that I couldn't get pumped, even though I was. I knew my forearms were rock hard, but my fingers latched on as strong as they had on the first holds, and I felt like I couldn't let go. In a way, I was glad that the Huber Pitch was so desperate because I found the upper dihedral crux comparatively far more certain. Still, it is a strenuous and relentless lead, and when I reached the anchor I was deeply worked. The wind was blowing hard at the belay, and I had the urge to leave the traverse pitch for the next day. The traverse wraps left, around the side of the Salathé Wall, and the rope runs around grainy arêtes. It is unbelievably exposed, and I found the powerful moves long and insecure, despite the big holds. I'd been freezing cold all day, and I wanted to rap to my sleeping bag. But the traverse was the final crux of the route, and it would be even harder to wake up sore and have to do it as a warm-up.

I made the big moves around the first arête, feeling like I was about to fall off every hold. This pitch, in keeping with the character of Free Rider, has a seemingly innocuous 12a rating, but it ends with a frightening off-balance and precarious undercling sequence, the last piece of gear out of sight around a gritty corner. In the back of my mind I feared that if I whipped off, the rope would shred on the rough arête and I would keep going straight down, thousands of feet to the Valley floor—good extra motivation not to fall. I was in a daze as I powered through the undercling section and climbed up to Round Table Ledge, and I didn't snap out of it as we rapped back down to the Block to sleep. It had been one of the best free climbing days of my life. Mentally, I was exhausted.

The next day was just a few steep crack pitches to the top. Although they weren't simple, I knew I could do them. Unless I dropped the rack or something . . . redpointing El Cap is so stressful! I pushed those thoughts aside, knowing I couldn't fall and that I would never let go of the rack till I was standing on top. It was a powerful feeling to be leading up the last flaring, bulging off-width with full confidence that I wouldn't fall. I remembered how demoralized I had been when I first tried it.

When we reached the top, I waited for a flood of triumph and was perplexed to feel nothing. The day before, firing the crux pitches, I had been exuberant. Yet now we were standing on top and I just felt tired. Was something wrong with me? Shouldn't I be jumping up and down, screaming and hearing the *Chariots of Fire* theme song as I ran around in slow motion? Instead, I mechanically coiled the ropes, reorganized the gear, packed the bag, and started down the East Ledges. I felt numb and drained. Suddenly, nothing mattered. For the last month every breath I took was for this climb. I'd been more driven than I'd ever been. Now it was over.

I became a hermit for many days, not talking to anyone except Fletcher. Finally I emerged and went to the Royal Arches, scampering light and free on warm rock. As I walked over the top of Washington Column, Half Dome appeared before me like an old friend, and suddenly it hit me: I had free climbed El Capitan through the force of my own effort. My eyes filled with tears.

Two weeks later, my friend Heinz came from Austria to shoot photos with me. I climbed the crux pitches and as we camped on top that night, Heinz said, "You looked great on those pitches. You should do it in a day." I have to admit, it had crossed my mind a time or two, maybe for next season. But Heinz meant now, after a few rest days. And he offered to jug for me. Almost the biggest crux last time was finding a partner. How could I turn down such an offer?

We walked to the base slowly, in the early evening. We had decided that I should start the Free Blast at 6:00 PM, giving me daylight for the insecure slab pitches. If I climbed fast, I could make it to Heart Ledge by dark and then start climbing by headlamp. Unfortunately it was a new moon, so I could depend only on my own light. I felt really nervous about climbing the Hollow Flake pitch in the dark. I didn't have that pitch very dialed. But I figured the Monster off-widths couldn't get much worse than usual, plus I could just pretend it was a nightmare. I was expecting to get to the Alcove by 6:00 AM, but Heinz insisted we would be there by 2:00 AM at the latest, and he put two superlight down sleeping bags in the pack.

We were a little early at the base, and as I organized my gear a young black bear silently approached. Heinz and I looked at him in delight. "A good sign!" we told each other, laughing, as he ambled off to the west.

At 5:45 I couldn't wait anymore, and I had to start climbing. I gave Heinz a big hug and set off. I was full of intense feelings—excitement and anxiety. This moment could be the beginning of a life-changing day, or we could soon be anticlimactically rapping in defeat. Well maybe not, we only had one rope. I decided that it was time to turn off my mind and to think only about climbing slowly and carefully, as both Dean and Thomas Huber had urged me to do. I knew it was sound advice. But after the slabby crux pitches, I started to wonder if I was climbing too slowly and carefully—I felt like I was barely moving. Much to my shock, as I started the final pitch of the Free Blast, Heinz told me that it had been only two hours since we left the ground.

As I finished the downclimb to Heart Ledge, I switched on my headlamps. Two Austrians were lying there in sleeping bags, a little surprised to see me. I looked at them enviously. I had a lot of climbing to do before I'd be in a sleeping bag. In full blackness, I started the next pitch. I was actually kind of enjoying climbing within my little circle of light. No distractions, the perfect temperature, nice and peaceful. And this business of having my own personal jugger, carrying the pack and all the extra gear—it was pretty deluxe! I carefully navigated up, across, and down, and started up the Hollow Flake. My rope flapped away into the darkness below, making this essentially a free solo. I felt calm as my nervousness was replaced by the familiar feeling of a big climbing push. Just keep on keeping on.

In some ways, I'd been training for this day for years. In my twenties, I'd been seduced by adventure and big climbs. I'd turned away from pushing pure free climbing difficulty to pursue new routes, big walls, and alpine experiences. Unfortunately, it's just not possible to be in top free climbing fitness when you're going on back-to-back expeditions. I never regretted my adventures for a moment, but two years ago I'd made the decision to halt my travels and really work at free climbing again. It's hard and frustrating to switch gears between climbing disciplines, but I've learned that past slogging and big pushes stay in there somewhere. My experiences in the mountains and on other big walls, moving endlessly, exhaustedly through the night, made me feel comfortable and relaxed now on El Cap as the hours rolled by. After all, there weren't even any scary conditions on this one—no storms, no loose rock, seracs, unknown regions above. As my nervousness subsided into the starry night, I realized that this was actually just fun!

Way up in the blackness, I groveled quietly up the Monster offwidths. The darkness hid the wild exposure, and I was surprised to feel totally relaxed, climbing much faster and more efficiently than I had hoped. Heinz was right, and we reached the Alcove around 2:00 or 3:00 AM. I put on the socks I'd brought and dozed until I woke shaking with cold at 5:30. It was hard to get going, and I was thankful I'd been smart enough to bring a little plastic bottle full of espresso. But it too was icy cold, more necessary than enjoyable. I tried to ignore the headache I'd had since starting the climb twelve hours before. How could I have forgotten aspirin? Probably just nerves, because I had no idea what was going to happen on the Huber Pitch. I did believe that if I could do it, I could do the route. If I couldn't do it . . . well, I had to do it.

At the base of the Huber Pitch, I gathered my energy and blocked all the lower pitches from my mind, pretending I really had slept a full night on the Alcove. With a shout, I stuck the jump move and cranked into the dihedral. Yes! As we reached the Block, Heinz started talking about the summit, still several cruxes away. Always a bad idea. Yet the first hard dihedral pitch felt shockingly easy—"5.9 for you!" Heinz shouted cheerfully. The next one was not as smooth. I was so cold that I had all my clothes on and foolishly kept my windbreaker on too. As I writhed up the slopey, funky corner, I felt myself slipping. Horrified, I started scrapping above the so-called protection (frayed pieces of tatty nylon cinched onto broken, knotted bashy cables) and somehow managed to fight to a stance. I'd spent far too much energy, and as I reached the end of the pitch, I felt myself actually falling out of a flared handjam. It's one of my cardinal rules that I never fall out of a handjam. Ever. In disbelief, I kept pulling and somehow landed my other hand in just as I

started to fall. At the belay I felt cold, exhausted, and mad at my inelegant performance. I hate it when I do stupid things, and I had just done several. The lack of sleep was getting to me. Irrationally, I expected to fall and somehow die on the next traverse pitch, but of course I didn't.

At Round Table Ledge, I just wanted to sleep. I like at least ten hours a night, and I'd only gotten three! I was grumpy and tired and didn't even feel like climbing the final three steep pitches to the top. I closed my eyes for a second and slumped against the wall until Heinz scolded me to keep going. Times like these, when it's just all tiredness, seem to be a part of every El Cap experience. In a way I didn't much care about the route anymore. I was detached and kind of apathetic, the classic victim of sleep deprivation. I envisioned pulling out my sleeping bag and dozing off, knowing that Heinz would never let me. That's the benefit of having a friend along on a big route rather than soloing—the luxury of fantasizing about laziness, knowing you can give in to weakness a little because your partner will yell at you until you move. But it didn't seem so great at the moment. I glanced at Heinz peevishly and started fussing with gear so I would at least look busy. Reorganizing the rack felt like a big hassle, and I grumbled silently to myself as I clipped carabiners and untangled slings. I finally got it together, and as soon as my hands sank into the next dihedral, I suddenly felt a flow of energy. Steep cracks! My favorite! I started running up the corner, laughing and feeling punchy. It had been about twenty hours since we left the ground, and everything was fun again.

We reached the top in the afternoon sun, and Heinz checked his watch: 4:00 PM on May 24, exactly one month since the last time I had topped out on Free Rider. I looked at Heinz, overwhelmed with gratitude, because he really had given this day to me, one of the best climbs of my life. I dropped the gear to the ground and stretched out in the sun, suffused with the contentment of exhaustion. Free Rider had pushed me in so many ways, further than any climb had pushed me before. As I sprawled on the warm granite slab, with no more left to do, I knew that I was not the same person who had stood at the foot of El Cap one long day before.

OPPOSITE: Upper dihedral, Free Rider, El Cap (photo by Heinz Zak)

9

LOVE DOGS

There are love dogs no one knows the names of.
Give your life to be one of them.
—Rumi

I WAS TORMENTED BY FITZROY, Patagonia's grandest peak, for so many years. It was a monkey on my back, a constant stab of inadequacy that I carried inside. Any success I had on other, more difficult climbs left me slightly dissatisfied, knowing that I'd put immeasurably greater effort into one mountain I still hadn't climbed—one that plenty of other people had. Disgrace definitely tinged my frustration.

I worried that not climbing the Fitz said something about me—I must not be trying hard enough, or not be good enough to get up the classic Patagonian summit. Fitzroy isn't the hardest peak in Patagonia, but it's the biggest and most impossible to ignore. With each season I put in down there, it ate away at me despite doing other climbs on other peaks. It seemed like something always got in the way—if not the weather, then logistics or timing or an alternate goal. It got to the point where it felt like I'd climbed almost everything *but* Fitzroy.

At a certain point, determination becomes derangement. After I finally laid the demon of desire to rest, I felt a lot of contradictions. As a person, I was remorseful about the selfish way I drove my climbing partner on Fitzroy, although as a climber, I approved of the unstoppable way I climbed. Mostly, I was scared when I recalled that for a brief period I actually didn't care if we got down. For a long time afterward,

OPPOSITE: Dean on the summit of Fitzroy, after his free solo first ascent of the California Roulette (photo by Dean Potter)

I was deeply afraid of ever wanting anything that much again, of being that ruthless person. It was many seasons before I would even take on a crag project, because of that fear.

But making peace with Fitzroy gave me release, and Dean too. He was on the mountain hours after I was. My girl-size crampon tracks in the snow seemed to whip him into an escalating speed-solo frenzy on Patagonia's highest peaks. He descended Fitzroy, raced up Cerro Torre, and then up Fitzroy again! Who knows where it all would have ended if he hadn't gotten nailed by a rock on the last descent, losing consciousness and then having to finish the rappels, crawl out over the glacier, and fly home to recover. At the next full moon, he showed up on my doorstep in Moab with a faint limp, a slightly ravaged thousand-yard stare, and a proposition of marriage. Gosh, who could say no?

My seven seasons in Patagonia have grown into a long-term relationship with that wild place. Patagonia suits a certain temperament. Some seasons are terrible, some are magical. Living in those mountains I find it impossible to believe that nature is impartial and unconnected. It's so tempestuous, so intense, so emotional. I think Patagonia has a sense of humor. It has been a harsh teacher but has finally pounded some lessons into my thick skull. I laugh to think of what a disastrous student I have been, but slowly and painfully I have grown to accept uncertainty. I have started to let go of the conviction that life should be "fair." I have learned to welcome the unknown.

Above all, I see that Patagonia gives you what you bring to it. A pure and silver mirror, the reflection is clear.

A LIFE OF PATAGONIA

Valentine's Day. Week nine in Patagonia. Day nine in a snow cave. Dean and I haven't spoken a word since we woke up. This is hands-down the most unromantic day of my life. I drop tears silently. I hate Dean. I hate Patagonia. I fantasize about being in a nice clean house, with a nice clean boyfriend who has just brought me a huge, lovely smelling bouquet of flowers. I am certain that at this very moment every girl in the Western world is wearing a dress and being showered with valentine gifts. I've been in this one-piece suit for months. Yesterday I took off my shell pants, and the coating was rotted out inside the crotch. I always thought that was just a figure of speech. Why am I here? I hate this snow cave. I hate myself. I hate everything. I can't believe I'm wasting my twenties like this. I lie corpselike in my damp sleeping bag and soak the top with

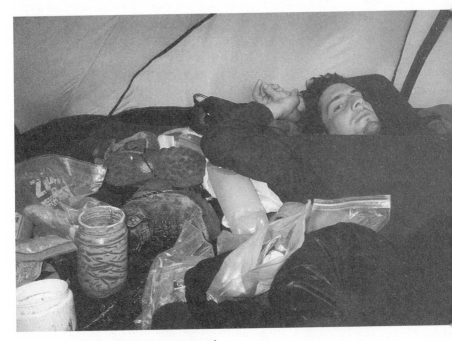

Festering in Patagonia (photo by Steph Davis)

tears, adding to the condensation problem and filling the bivy tent with a cloud of misery and self-pity. Dean is comatose. I can't even imagine good weather anymore.

When we arrived in Patagonia two and a half months ago, Dean and I vowed enthusiastically that we wouldn't leave until we had summited Fitzroy, the jewel of the Fitzroy range. We remained ruthlessly optimistic for months, crossing the glacier in full whiteouts and climbing even in storms, knowing we wouldn't summit but getting tougher. We dug in our heels as all the other climbers bailed out of this unbelievably worthless Patagonia season. The weather responded by continuously growing so bad that eventually we couldn't even get farther than our snow cave at Paso Superior, high at the edge of the glacier on the east side of Fitzroy.

We are on the edge of insanity. We have managed not to kill each other, but just barely. We hole up in the snow cave for one last-ditch siege, knowing that when we run out of food and fuel we will cede defeat to this ultimately crappy year.

The food is nearly gone when the weather suddenly breaks. We almost can't comprehend sun and blue sky. The granite peaks are in clear view at last, completely encrusted with ice. Dazed and panicked, we snap into action and decide to climb a rock route on Mermoz while Fitzroy melts off. But after postholing across the glacier in snowshoes and wallowing up a snowfield, we find the cracks choked with snow and ice. Of course they are; they've been bombarded for the last three months.

We trudge back to the snow cave, with the sinking knowledge that the good weather could end at any moment, but everything is far too out of condition to climb. We take stock of our meager food supplies and decide that our only hope is the Supercanaleta, on the northwest side of Fitzroy, almost directly opposite where we are on this side of the range. The route is mostly snow, so there's a chance that we could climb it in these conditions. It's true that we're on the wrong side of the mountain, and we don't know anything about the route. If the Supercanaleta isn't climbable tomorrow, we will have wasted all our remaining food and a lot of energy trying to get there, and maybe the weather window as well. But the other choice is to stay at the snow cave and wonder if it could have worked. We decide to take the gamble, to find our way around the mountains, postholing across the high glacier in snowshoes under heavy packs.

As we circumnavigate the peaks, passing around Mermoz and Guillaumet, I start to enjoy this movement into unfamiliar territory under clear skies. We make a lucky guess at which pass to use on the north and drop down steep snowfields for thousands of feet to the glacier on Fitzroy's northeast side. We're moving fast, trying to finish this journey before dark, when I fall into a crevasse up to my armpits. I writhe like a beetle under my pack, desperately flailing until I can crawl away from the cracked edges. Rattled and panting, I lie on the ice for a few seconds. Dean waits impatiently as I struggle back to my feet, the rope tugging insistently between us. In the fading light, we can see the end of the glacier, barren and desolate, with no hope of shelter.

Snow starts to fall lightly. We huddle beside a small boulder on the ice and struggle into the single bivy sack. As the snow and wind intensify, we endure a wet, freezing night. I spend the hours trying to wiggle my toes inside my boots, but my legs are crushed against Dean's in the narrow one-person sack. Snow blows into the top of the bivy and melts down our faces, soaking the wafer-thin sleeping bag that we are also crammed into. We are both wondering if we are going to get slammed by a massive storm way out here alone, with almost no food or shelter. The night drags on forever as I try to ignore the pain in my cramped legs, shivering and yearning for the snow cave.

By morning the storm dribbles out into the fresh hope of another clear day. Gratefully, we extract our aching limbs from the torture sack and trudge up to the base of Fitzroy. I am beaten down, but I know I have the drive to climb this huge mountain, if we can just get the chance. Since we have no information, we are pleasantly surprised to see the route is dead obvious. A huge snow gully starts right off the glacier, indeed a Super Couloir. We stand before it and look up. Unbelievably, the Supercanaleta is totally out of condition too. The entire upper portion of rock, thousands of feet, is coated in rime. We could climb the lower portion of the route on snow, but there would be no chance of making it to the summit. We've had enough of that game already.

Almost completely out of food, we've run ourselves ragged. The gamble didn't pay off, which pretty much sums up this entire season.

It takes hours to retrace our circuit around the mountains, back up to the snow cave on the east glacier. Hungry and drained, we try to figure out some way to salvage this miserable trip. Dean spots a dihedral high

Open bivy below the Supercanaleta, Fitzroy (photo by Steph Davis)

on Poincenot that appears to have melted out in the last two days, with a long couloir leading up to the rock. The weather still seems good. It's not Fitzroy, and in fact the last peak we climbed together last season was Poincenot, but at this point we have to get up something. We have six Clif Bars left and a little bit of dehydrated soup. Beyond exhaustion, we try to nourish our haggard bodies with the soup and we zip the precious Clif Bars in the pack.

As darkness falls, we are out on snowshoes again, trudging toward Poincenot. Dean and I simulclimb snow and ice all night, moving more quickly in tandem than if we were stopping to belay each other. We reach the col as dawn breaks. Unbelievably, the rock above is dry, and it has good crack systems. As we climb, we find no anchors and suspect a new route. We are both praying the line doesn't suddenly fade out, forcing a retreat from an insurmountable blank face. Retreat would be awful, leaving all of our gear for anchors and having to downclimb all the ice we climbed up through the night. We packed as light as we could, bringing almost no clothing, and we are incredibly cold and almost out of reserves, but we won't stop until we are standing on a summit.

The hours slip by, and we finally reach the summit. But it's just a brief moment of relief, and then we're rappeling off the other side of Poincenot. Night catches us as we touch the glacier. We are so relieved to have climbed something, anything, and we are truly exhausted.

Back down in El Chalten, we eat frantically and tell the locals of our climb. They tell us we have done a first ascent. It's hard to get too excited about it, when all we wanted to climb was Fitzroy. We summited Poincenot already last year, on the Whillans Route, so despite the cachet of the new route our climb actually seems like a cruel joke after these three brutal months here. This is my fourth trip to Patagonia and my second time here with Dean. We are no strangers to rough living, maddening weather, and the irritability that comes with them. Even when we are not in the mountains, we have lived nomadically in vehicles, tents, and caves for the last five years and have always been a tempestuous pair. But after this relentless season, it feels like something has been irreparably damaged. It's too much. We don't even like each other anymore. We fly back to the States, to separate vehicles, and drive off in different directions.

———————|———————

Failure is irresistible. Dean and I decide within a few months to return to Patagonia together. Still, when push comes to shove, neither one of us can fully get over how spectacularly wretched the last trip was. Our insecure relationship just adds to the complication and makes it nearly impossible to plan anything. We both get overwhelmed by anxiety and split up, yet again, a couple months before it's time to leave. Well, this drama has gone on for years, and my main concern at the moment is the lack of a Patagonia partner. I scramble to find a new climbing partner, realizing with some annoyance that Dean and I will both be there this winter and could even find ourselves on the same climb. This makes everything seem more than a little ridiculous, but clearly we can't function together at this point, even though we both want to do exactly the same things. We're both so driven, it seems impossible to reconcile our ambitions. But who else would be able to handle either one of us? This will have to be dealt with. But not right now.

I let it be known that my base will be the east side of Fitzroy, not sure if I hope Dean will pick the west or the east when he hears my intentions. I'm absolutely 100 percent sure that this is the year I will finally climb Fitzroy. I'm sure that if I give in to the setbacks and don't go, it will turn out to be the best weather year in history and everyone will climb everything and I will have to commit seppuku. I know with unshakable clarity that I need to find a partner, any partner, and get down there. I'm not even very perturbed when the partner I do find gets injured and has to bail out on me the day before we are to leave the country. My bags are packed and I'm going. I'm more determined than I've ever been in my life. I leave the States four days before Christmas, and Fitzroy is the only thing I care about.

By Christmas Eve I'm in Argentina and have moved expedition bags and myself to the Poincenot base camp, on the east side of Fitzroy. It's

OPPOSITE: Fitzroy from the east side, white with rime ice (photo by Steph Davis)

only ten minutes away from the more traditional climbers' base camp that Dean and I used last year, but I can't bring myself to live there this season. Besides, this camp is a little farther out from the peaks and allows me to see them when they're not choked in flying clouds. The only other people here are two very cheerful Austrian climbers who had the same thought and have been based at this camp trying for Fitzroy for a month. As I pitch my tents, they wander over and invite me to share their gummy Christmas pasta. We eat from a scratched plastic bowl under the branches of a lean-to shelter, and the Austrians tell me stories about sparkling yuletide celebrations at home in Austria, instead of inside this dank, lonely forest.

After about ten minutes, Alex and Wolfgang also invite me to join them if they get another chance for Fitzroy. Although I have a reputation for being a competent Patagonia climber by now, my fifth time here, I'm still amazed by their generosity. They're both strong climbers, a good team, and have been high on the Franco-Argentine Route already in marginal weather. The addition of an unknown third could only be a liability for them if we got to try the route, but they are absolutely sincere in their invitation. Unfortunately for me, this is the last week of their time here. We are theoretically a team for the week, but the weather is never good enough to leave base camp, and then the Austrians are gone.

Fortunately, within another ten minutes I meet a German climber, Philip. He's also here alone, rather spontaneously, and has heard that I'm looking for a partner for Fitzroy, which he too would like to climb. Climbers are starting to arrive here now from other areas, and friends report that they met Philip on the slopes of Aconcagua and in the granite peaks of Bariloche, and that he's a good climber. He tells me he climbs in the Alps. He has two arms and two legs, speaks English, and is kind to small animals. That's all I know. It's enough.

After a few days, the weather improves, allowing us to make the three-hour snow slog up to Paso Superior to check out the snow cave the Austrians have bequeathed us. It's a pretty grim little hole, nothing like the suite Dean and I created in months of inactivity last season.

For the next two weeks, the weather is flat-out bad. Philip and I go up a couple times and renovate our cave. More climbers start to show up, and we all sit around, eating and drinking and wandering around the forests. To me, at this point, two weeks of bad weather is like the blink of an eye, so I am stunned when Philip sits me down and tells me that he can't stand waiting for good weather for much longer. "But it's only been two weeks!" I protest uselessly. I can't believe he would be so flighty. He can't believe I would rather fester in this cold, wet forest than go somewhere you can actually climb. I realize that if the weather breaks even a little, we will need to go for Fitzroy immediately, as it will be my only chance before being partnerless again.

The weather starts looking slightly better. Philip tells me that he'll go up to the snow cave for the last time. Either we'll climb, or he'll carry his gear down. We start walking as night falls, and I turn my brain off for the familiar uphill slog. Sometimes I wonder how many times I've toiled up this hill, but thinking about it only makes it worse.

We reach the snow cave during the night and decide that this is our last-ditch, now-or-never moment. It's the right time of night to start out for the climb, and the weather isn't terrible. I sense that if we don't go now, Philip will be walking down in the morning. We gear up and continue onto the glacier. The only problem is that I'm tired from getting up here and from all the aimless hiking up random talus slopes I did in the last several boring days. Philip seems buzzed from the walk and feels strong, so I gratefully take the back end of the rope and let him break trail across the glacier. My legs feel sore, and my pack feels heavy. This isn't how I want to be starting Fitzroy, but this is a chance and must not be wasted.

We start simulclimbing the snow slopes that lead to the Italian Breccia, a col high on the mountain, and I'm still tired. This angle of snow always makes me a little grouchy—it's repetitive and interminably calf-burning, easy but just dangerous enough to keep me slightly on edge. It seems that my life has degenerated into slogging, and I wonder how this has happened to me. So unglamorous. So not like rock climbing . . . so why do I keep ending up like this? This is the kind of thing I should be doing when I'm old and can't rock climb. Just when I'm at the height of my silent complaints, the snow gets steep and icy and traversing, and I slam my ice tools in hard, momentarily terrified instead of tired. Ah, Patagonia.

Icy rock on the Franco-Argentine, Fitzroy (Steph Davis collection)

I switch to real climbing mode and start up a mixed pitch of rock, ice, and snow, falling onto the anchor when rock breaks under my cammed ice pick. Oops. Morning breaks as we reach the breccia, the actual "start" of the Franco-Argentine Route, although we have already been climbing for hours. It's looking like this will actually be a good day. Still, it's pretty ridiculous to be up here on the first clear day after a month of storms. I don't see how the route could be in any condition for climbing, but here we are. We make our way up more snow and find the first rock pitch of the Franco-Argentine. It's a splitter crack, and it's absolutely packed full of snow and ice. Philip looks at it doubtfully, saying it's too snowy to climb. I offer to start, change to rock shoes, and get set for a big cleaning festival. The sun makes the snow soft and pretty easy to pull out from the crack. No doubt the route will be in perfect shape tomorrow.

Two Americans I know have arrived at the base behind us, and they wait patiently as I scrape the snow and ice out of the first pitch with my nut tool. I'm glad that at least the crack will be in shape for the others, because it makes the slow cleaning work feel more productive, like community service. I keep climbing, as the crack systems start turning into waterspouts and then waterfalls.

I'm first surprised, then astonished at the sheer volume of fixed line hanging down every pitch. It's as if some psychotic, gargantuan spider lost control of its web-making function and spewed nylon strands all over Fitzroy. Most of it is just in the way, and I've heard story after story of climbers taking huge whippers or dying from trusting fixed anchors or ropes in Patagonia. Occasionally, I theoretically trust a fixed line as protection to try to make some time, leaving Philip to ascend my lead rope with jumars as I run out another pitch with the tag line, clipping the thin static rope to nests of fixed line along the way. It probably wouldn't do anything for a lead fall, but it gives me enough confidence to keep moving as Philip jugs, getting us higher.

We aren't going fast, but we're going. We're both getting pretty wet, and I'm leading with a pack on to get some weight off of Philip who, being from the Alps rather than Yosemite, is not finding Yosemite-style jumaring to be fast or efficient. But I'm exhilarated that we're actually climbing on Fitzroy. This is the first time I have actually set a rock shoe on this mountain since my very first trip to Patagonia, when Charlie and I nearly got up it and then nearly didn't get off it. I am determined not to go down unless we have stood on top.

As the day rolls on, Philip is getting tired. He's not used to climbing in bad conditions and doesn't really understand why we're still up here. "Isn't it bad sometimes in the Alps?" I ask, perplexed. I can't think of a time I've climbed in Patagonia in good conditions. "If it is like this in the Alps," he tells me, "I just go home." I'm starting to worry a little. Philip seems less and less psyched. We're wet, and clouds are rolling in. The ropes are soaked from the waterspouts and are hard to handle, knotting constantly. I ask Philip to switch jobs, thinking that he might actually find leading less physical than jumaring, as he is not used to the technique and seems to be wearing out. We swap gear, and he heads up a crack. After two pitches we're off route, and I reach him at a small ledge. We are no more than three pitches below the final snow slope that will take us to the summit.

Philip looks at me, and at the stormy late sky, and starts pouring out his exhaustion. "Steph, I have to say honestly, I am at my limit. I am too tired. I cannot go any farther. We have to go down!" I am aghast. It doesn't seem possible to be this close and want to go down. It will be epic no matter what at this point. Why not stick it out for another hour or two and make the summit before having to suffer through the descent? Frantically, I cajole, convince, insist, beg, demand. Philip is adamant. Finally I hit on the inarguable point that it would be easier to descend if we got back on route first, snatch back the gear, and start up a steep icy crack, trying to get over toward the right, where we should be. The rope runs out as I reach a ledge, so I fix the line for Philip and look up to see how much farther we have to go.

To my relief, I see we are back on route, and the top of the rock section is just above me, only about a rope length away. Just past there, we will be running up snow to the summit. Another rope hangs down, the end dangling fifteen feet above my stance. I recognize it as the end of the Americans' tag line, rather than yet another abandoned fixed rope. They have been close behind us all day and got ahead during our little detour. I imagine the guys up there, with just a little bit of snow to climb to the summit, and yearn to be up there with them.

Dusk is coming, and Philip seems to be jugging the pitch as slowly as possible in hopes I will just give up and let us rappel. Waiting starts to feel like torture. I search below, expecting to see him at any second. It seems impossible to jug this slowly. I know with a sick certainty that when he reaches me he will absolutely insist on going down, essentially one pitch away from summiting. There might never be another chance . . . somehow five years have passed since the first time I tried to climb this thing. Now that I'm actually here again, and this close, you'd have to smash my fingers one by one with an ice hammer to pry me off. How could Philip have known? I look so normal.

I try to calm my mind and to wait Zen-like to see what happens. An hour goes by. It is simply not humanly possible to take this long to jumar one pitch! My lead rope is still weighted; is he conscious? I'm in misery. The dusk is growing. Suddenly I'm certain that Philip is intentionally staying out of sight until darkness falls, not moving, to force our descent. He refuses to go up, I refuse to go down. He has the lead rope weighted and out of commission, and right now Philip seems to have me checkmated. This partnership has dissolved into a battle of wills. I appear to be at a slight disadvantage, since Philip is on the same team as gravity. I will not let this climb fall apart.

I think fast. I suspect that if I can force Philip a little higher, up to the snow and off the hated jumars, he might rally. If I get off the lead line and lead out on the tag line while he's still jugging the lead line, as I'd been doing lower on the route to make time, Philip could arrive at the belay and tie it off on me before I reached the anchor. Would he do that? Impossible to predict at this point. My mind flies, shuffling the data like a hard drive. We are not going down.

I start shouting up through the wind. "HEY! YOU GUYS!! Can you hear me?? Can you lower your rope five feet and pull up my tag rope on your line??!! HEY!! Lower your rope a little!!!" It's so windy, they may not hear me, they may not even be there, and I will have wasted these seconds that I could have been starting up the pitch with a self-belay. But if they do hear me, I will eliminate any possibility of being made to go down, because if I'm gone when Philip reaches the ledge, with no trailing rope to stop me, he'll have no choice but to come up the last pitch. Suddenly the rope comes down a few feet. With numbed hands, I tie my wet skinny tag line to it, give it a tug, and watch as it quickly flies up.

Philip seemed absolutely exhausted and desperate when he'd insisted we go down, but after these weeks together I know he's actually quite strong. Still, I don't truly know what he's capable of at this point. With someone I knew, it would be acceptable—and even an act of good partnership—to push them past their mental limits. But I don't know Philip, and truthfully I'm thinking more about myself and how badly I need to go up. On one hand, I think it's wrong to push someone past their limits in the mountains. But I think it's even more wrong to go to pieces under pressure in the mountains, becoming a liability for your partner. In a way, I find being backed into this corner to be terribly unfair, as I have pulled far more than my weight already—an arguably self-centered perspective.

I struggle for a second with my conscience, but only for a second. Numbly I realize I don't care about anything beyond this climb. For five years, this has been the only thing I have really wanted. I quickly make old-school prusiks with pieces of cord and start pushing them up the soaked 7-millimeter cord as I climb up the rock, belaying myself in this way, climbing as fast as I can so that if Philip suddenly appears at the ledge I won't be close enough to talk to. The truth is, nothing anyone could say would make me go down now.

When I reach the shoulder, the two Americans look at me, obviously trying to figure out what the hell is going on down there. I thank them somewhat incoherently, explaining to them that I had to put an irreversible move on Philip, that he wanted to bail. They are on their first trip here and just summited Fitzroy. I can tell they don't understand the depth of my dysfunctional relationship with this mountain, and they think I'm a little whacked. Well, yeah. The wind and snow kick up as they rig their rappel lines. I wait for Philip and pull up the lead rope when he reaches the belay ledge below me. Ooooh, it doesn't sound good! I hear shouts and screams as he pushes himself past his limit, jumaring the wet rope.

When Philip gets to me it's almost dark, and the ropes are starting to freeze and stiffen. "You're doing awesome Philip, it's only half an hour now up the snow," I say, bracing myself for his fury. Philip looks at me. He smiles. "I'm totally calm now," he says. "I don't even care anymore. I feel fine. We will summit!" He is jubilant.

We change into our wet boots and crampons. Philip clips his pack to the last anchor and rushes up the snowfield. I dig his headlamp out of the lid and put it over my neck with my own. Suddenly drained, now I try to keep up with him, breathing hard and kicking into the snow. He is as strong as I thought; the exhaustion really was all in his mind, and he just broke through. My calves ache dully. We are almost there.

Above in the dark mist, I can see a black mound with nothing higher. I can feel Philip's joy, the tangible thrill of his triumph, and I catch a buzz from his elation. I know how extraordinary it feels to believe that you are physically done and then suddenly find that you are even stronger. I did

Philip and I on the summit of Fitzroy (photo by Steph Davis)

the right thing after all, but the truth is that we are strangers and I had no way of knowing Philip would break through his mental barrier. Even if forcing him up to the snow turned out to be the right thing, I probably did it for the wrong reasons. Things could have gone terribly wrong, and I would have been completely to blame. I'm going to brood over my ruthlessness for a long time after this, but in this moment everything is magnificent. We stop just below the top. I'm crying now. "Philip, I can't believe it, I can't believe it."

"You go first," Philip says happily. I go up. It's all clouds, the light is completely gone. No view whatsoever. We're on the summit of Fitzroy. After all these years. Finally.

I sob and laugh and hug Philip. I'm so relieved we're here and that he doesn't hate me. My ruthless, machinelike drive is gone, and now I fear deeply that he will be angry with me. Philip smiles and hugs me back. "Now we have to go slow and be really careful going down," he says. It's unbelievable how completely he has recovered from his exhaustion and panic, and even more unbelievable that he seems to have forgotten it completely. He is absolutely solid. And too mild to hold a grudge. I am hit by a rush of affection and respect.

We are silent, wet and cold, making our way down the gray snow by headlamp. When we reach our anchor, the slings are frozen, the ropes are frozen, and the wind is blowing snow and sleet through the blackness. But it doesn't matter. It doesn't matter at all.

We start the rappels, fighting the frozen, tangled ropes, and eventually stop to spend the night sitting cloaked beneath a thin bivy sack on a small pointed rock, partially hanging in our harnesses. The bivy sack keeps the snow off but ices up inside from condensation. I wiggle my wet feet for hours, crammed up against Philip under the sack, feeling only pure cold as we wait for dawn.

The morning breaks clear. We continue down during the nicest day I've yet seen in Patagonia. Above us, the rock is now melted out and nearly dry. No waterfalls, a perfect climbing day. I don't even care that we had to suffer in bad conditions, forcing it a day early. We reached the top, and I thank this day for being what it is—a calm clear day to get off the mountain and down to safety.

Much later we come down from Paso Superior, off the final snows, stumbling down the last stretch of steep rocky trail to Poincenot Camp. Philip and I are both euphoric. We seem to be moving in synch, in smooth partnership at last. Throughout the entire descent, especially after the long hours of last night's shivering bivy, we have drawn close, feeling more and more connected. Neither of us will forget our intense experience and the ways in which we pushed each other. We have brought down only Philip's gear from the snow cave, because I am still hoping to climb more, if I can find a new partner. . . . For now, we will descend to El Chalten and celebrate together.

As my eyes leave the white and gray of the snowy terrain and meet the blue and green expanse below, everything looks so beautiful, bathed in filtered cinematic light. I am filled with what I can only articulate as pure ecstasy. I have never felt this way before and don't expect I ever will again. I am finally free, and the whole world feels like love. I have never been this happy.

Dawn on the east-side glacier, Patagonia (photo by Dean Potter)

TORRE EGGER

Evening. White snow, gray shadows, blue figures. Calm and cold on the silent glacier. Cerro Torre, Torre Egger, and Cerro Standhardt loom ahead, quiet gray cathedrals, making us small. A thousand little footsteps trail behind, ant tracks, temporary record of our passage.

The rope draws snake marks between us. Dean and I wend around crevasses and depressions, approaching Torre Egger. It's a familiar state of being, stepping together across white fields. Connected by a hundred feet of rope, we match our pace to keep the line taut, watching for crevasses.

Only a few days ago we were almost on the top of Torre Egger. We had climbed the Titanic route all the way to the gigantic snow mushroom that hangs over the mountain's top. These mushrooms are the strangest things I've ever encountered. I don't think they exist anywhere but on these torres, or if they do, I've never heard about it. Wet and cold, we huddled below the mushroom on a sloping fin of rock until the darkest morning hours, holding the stove in our hands to make broth, waiting for the snow to firm up enough to hold ice picks and crampons. A good strategy, but it was a strangely warm weather window and the snow would not freeze hard enough to climb. The mushroom, a giant sloughing snow cone, dumped cartloads of wet snow over us as we rappeled in defeat, one agonizing rope length below the summit. A couple days of storm, then another weather window opened almost immediately, before we could recover our energy.

Being turned back only meters from the summit just sharpens our determination. We are still worked over from the first effort, but we have to try again. Knowing the route this time, we decide to climb Yosemite speed-style, hoping to make the first one-day ascent of Torre Egger. Only five teams have ever summited Torre Egger, compared to hundreds or maybe thousands that have climbed its taller neighbor, Cerro Torre—the

OPPOSITE: View of Cerro Torre and Torre Egger, from Cerro Standhardt (photo by Dean Potter)

bolted Compressor Route makes Cerro Torre a quick jaunt for strong climbers with good weather. There is no easy way up Torre Egger. It is an intimidating mountain.

This weather window opens cold and clear, good mushroom weather, and we understand more about the route's personality. We decide to climb most of it in the night, avoiding the waterfalls that dumped over us last time, to reach the mushroom during the coldest time of morning. No bivy this time, just constant motion. For speed climbing Dean is definitely the faster leader, and we agree that he will lead the whole route, short-fixing and simulclimbing when necessary, rather than wasting time by switching belays and swapping lead blocks. If Dean leads a pitch even just five minutes faster than me, over thirty pitches that adds up to two and a half hours of time savings. This way we can bring just one pair of crampons, one set of ice tools, and only Dean's rock shoes, saving a lot of weight, and we also eliminate any changeover time.

The main advantage of leading in blocks on a big route, switching leaders after several pitches, is to give the leader a chance to recover from the pressure of being on the sharp end, but Dean is one of the strongest climbers I know and he doesn't need the break. It's also true that I can jug like a machine under a pack, for hours on end, and I'm probably even a bit faster at it than Dean. So with a speed-style ascent as our goal, this plan makes sense. Mentally it's hard for me to take "the back seat," despite our logical reasons for this strategy. In reality, it's a hard job—carrying the heavy pack, managing the ropes, jugging continuously. In the mountains, with a serious objective, each person has to do whatever will make the team fastest. There is no room for ego.

Dean and I stand on the lip of a little bergschrund, at the base of Torre Egger. Last time we were filled with the mystery and anticipation of an unknown route. This time, we know everything that lies ahead. We are physically still tired from our last effort, mentally not as engaged, but it is important to us to finish what we started. We both have absolutely no expectation of even reaching the summit—we have climbed too much in Patagonia and we know how fast things change. The truth is that climbing the rather chossy rock on this route again is not completely appealing, but the idea of reaching the top of this notorious mountain in one day is inspiring.

Dean starts climbing, and when I hear his shout I start moving. When I reach the first anchor he's already fifty feet up the next pitch, the huge loop of rope he's pulled up and fastened to the anchor to short-fix getting smaller as he climbs. I hurriedly free his rope from the anchor, put him on belay, and a few minutes later am jugging again. It's satisfying to move so efficiently together. Darkness falls and we switch on our headlamps, keeping the pace.

It's a little eerie, climbing through the silent Patagonia night. I've battled so many storms here that stillness seems almost menacing, somehow not quite right. But the darkness is also comforting. Dean and I find peace when we are living in our own private reality, alone in the mountains. Being here feels natural and right, and that's why we strive so hard to enter these moments, where desire is pure, simple, a clear balance between effort and acceptance. My mind is full of Torre Egger. I feel a contemplative sense of supplication, but without expectation.

Hours pass. We force ourselves to eat energy bars, though we have almost no water. Hunger dies, replaced by an intellectual decision to take in calories. Short night fades to dawn, and the rock stays dry and cold. We know we have to hurry, because we are in the water zone, below the mushroom. If the day starts to warm, we will get soaked, so we try to keep pushing. Dean is unstoppable, at his best when free soloing, which is the mentality he needs for the speed-style method of short-fixing, leading off the anchors with a huge loop of rope while I am still jugging the pitch below, placing the most minimal protection in order to keep moving without stopping to get gear back from me. For pitch after pitch, we never stop to meet, until he is completely out of gear and we both catch a needed break while we reorganize.

We climb fast over one or two thousand feet, impossible to measure as we rush past anchors. The night lightens, giving us energy. We reach the angling section high up on the route, a few pitches of traversing. This is fairly easy rock, so we start climbing together. In my mountain boots, it's awkward and a little difficult, and I have to concentrate hard to make sure I don't fall and pull Dean off.

Simulclimbing demands the highest level of trust, and Dean and I climb this way a lot. When simulclimbing, if the bottom person falls the leader can be pulled off the rock, usually with very little protection gear, and will probably get severely injured. So, unlike a normal climbing situation, the bottom person has twice as much responsibility not to fall. Our extreme size difference works to our advantage, because we always simulclimb with me on the bottom. Since I am so much lighter and since Dean is unusually strong, we theorize that if the unthinkable happens and I fall, Dean might have the strength to hang on and not be pulled off by my weight. According to us, simulclimbing is actually safer for us than for more evenly sized people, so we can do it on relatively difficult terrain that might otherwise be considered unsafe for simuling. Fortunately, this theory has never actually been tested, but it gives us the confidence to move fast together.

After only fifteen hours of climbing, the snow mushroom comes into sight just a few hundred feet above us. We are satisfied at how quickly we've gotten here. We are tired, but mostly dry, and optimistic that the mushroom will be firm enough to climb this time. Also, we have a better plan. After our failure last time, Dean spent some time studying the overhanging mushroom through a spotting scope from base camp. Much to our chagrin, he noticed an easier-looking path to the summit, veering around to the west below the mushroom before heading up it on better terrain. Possibly, we could have summited the first time had we discovered this other option. But now, with colder conditions and a smarter line, our chances are good.

We reach our previous bivy "ledge" in the morning light. I am happy to be climbing away from the sharp, granular fin that sticks out of the snow like a downward-sloping surfboard angling toward the long drop-off below, and I laugh a little at what a miserable bivy spot it was. We are right below the bulging mushroom, the terrain has changed to snow and ice, and I am still jugging, cramponless.

Dean climbs up soft snow, then moves left to a ridge. The other side is ice, and he traverses with ice tools and crampons several meters left and down to reach a rock ledge. When I get to the ridge, still on jumars, I look over, perplexed. If I just cut loose from here, I will fall down and to the left, slamming into the rock wall below him. I have no ice gear. I don't know how to get over there without getting hurt. Finally, Dean clips his ice tools to the rope and I reel them in. Keeping the jumars on the horizontal rope, I try to traverse over with the ice tools, but without crampons my feet skate wildly as I hang one-armed off the tools. It isn't going to work. Even if I could manage one-armed campus moves with the ice tools, I would need a third hand to slide the jumars to protect myself. I thrash back to the safety of the snow, frustrated and kind of baffled. Suddenly I figure it out, plant a tool in the ice, and clip my aider to it. I stand on it, then whack in the next tool and step over onto it. Oh right, ice aiding! A technique I will probably never use again, but it works perfectly. Dean looks relieved, but I mentally kick myself for not being quick enough to think of it immediately, wasting time and energy.

Things are starting to slow down. We are getting closer to the twenty-four-hour mark. Late afternoon. Dean switches back to rock mode, and then back to ice again, finally cresting the mushroom with a shout of triumph. I jug up the steep blue ice to find him perched on a downsloping snowfield. It is a strangely small place, the top of the mushroom. It is flat enough to sit on but angled enough to feel a little insecure, especially without crampons. I would hate to fall off the top of Torre Egger. The true summit is a soft point of snow, one more rope length up. Like some of the more crumbly desert towers in Moab, there is no way to get up or down it except by climbing. Dean climbs up and stands on the rather precarious point, then climbs back down and gives me the tools and crampons so I can summit too. The sky is crystal blue, and the sun warms us. We are pleased to have fulfilled our goal together, but we are far from finished. We organize the gear, putting off the inevitable.

The only way to get off this mushroom is to rappel off snow pickets or a stuff sack. We left pickets on the summit mushroom of Standhardt two weeks ago, sweating as we hung in space, willing the pickets not to slice out of the snow. This time we brought a stuff sack instead—lighter and, according to our European friends, much more solid than pickets in soft snow—but we've never rappeled off one before. In fact, we've never asked this nylon bag to do more than store our tent, but now it's the only way off this mountain. With the ice tools we dig a deep trench

Dean rappeling Torre Egger (photo by Steph Davis)

and fill the bag with snow. When the stuff sack is dense and fat, we sling a cord around it and entomb it deep for our anchor, letting the cord run out of a groove through the snow. We spend almost an hour slapping and punching the snow, compacting it, knowing that at some point we will have to call it good and hang all of our body weight off this thing on a free-hanging rappel from the top of Torre Egger. It's probably solid enough to hold a truck by the time we're done, but I can't help imagining it being pulled up out of the snow as I rap the dangling ropes.

As it grows dark, we are several pitches down on the granite. Finally it happens: I pull the rope, and the free end catches on something above us. We flick it, then pull it, then clip jumars to it and throw our bodies backward. The rope doesn't budge. We look at each other, dulled. At this point we have been going for about thirty hours. Dean makes a desultory attempt to climb up and concedes it's not worth the risk. Neither one of us really wants to deal with it, and since it's not storming, we decide we don't have to. We crouch beside each other on spiky rocks and shiver until morning, our light two-person bivy sack pulled over us like a tent. I nod off, then jerk awake and wiggle my toes inside my boots, then nod off again. Condensation freezes, coating the inside of the bivy sack with thin frost. We are thankful for the bit of warmth the sack gives us, glad we chose to bring it instead of the stove.

When morning comes at last, we can see the rope is irretrievably caught, high up and to the right of the route. We cut it free and rappel with what we have left, making ridiculously short rappels, leaving slings and nuts behind. It goes on and on, the endless travel down. Finally we reach the snow and stagger down to the rock slabs above our camp, the Norwegos Bivouac. We drop flat and greedily suck from the water that runs down the slabs.

The little bivy tent at high camp has never felt so comfortable and warm. Too tired to sleep or even eat, we lie next to each other listening to trance music, two pairs of headphones plugged into an MP3 player. I've listened to this Oakenfold hundreds of times, but it seems like I've never actually heard it before. I am completely absorbed, noticing every tone, every beat. It seems like the most amazing sound I've ever heard. I have the feeling that I will remember this state for the rest of my life. I wonder if Dean is sleeping or if he feels it too. Eyes closed, I listen to the music.

10

GOING IN

By performing asanas, the disciple first gains health, which is not mere existence. It is not a commodity which can be purchased with money. It is an asset to be gained by sheer hard work. It is a state of complete equilibrium of body, mind and spirit. Forgetfulness of physical and mental consciousness is health.

—B. K. S. Iyengar

It is by the coordinated and concentrated efforts of the body, senses, mind, reason and self that one obtains the prize of inner peace and fulfills the quest of the soul to meet its Maker. The supreme adventure in a person's life is the journey back to the Creator.

—B. K. S. Iyengar

I NEVER THOUGHT IN MY WILDEST DREAMS that one day I would free climb the Salathe Wall, one of the most inspiring of all rock climbs.

As a climber, I have always felt like the pesky little sister chasing after the older, faster, bigger kids. I came from an academic suburban background, hardly exposed to athletics or outdoor pursuits. When I hit the road, gripped by an inescapable passion for climbing and wild places, I had no immediate role models or feeling of support. But for some reason I charged on, trying to learn, trying to get better, trying to hang with my new friends who all seemed so skilled and so far ahead. That feeling only intensified when I met Dean, who has more natural physical and creative gifts than I've ever seen in one person.

Since the day I met him, Dean has insisted that he can do anything

OPPOSITE: The enduro pitch, Salathe Wall (photo by Jimmy Chin)

he envisions. And much to my amazement, I've seen over and over that he does! He also insists that I can too. For me, it has been hard to let go of attachments, hard to let go of self-doubt.

But slowly I'm starting to understand that it's not just a fluke when I succeed. And I'm starting to realize that in climbing, as in life, determination and a commitment to learning are qualities as invaluable as unusually strong body parts. Persistence and fanatical hard work are powerful assets not to be underestimated. I brought all my drive and more discipline than I knew I had to freeing the Salathe . . . and it almost wasn't enough.

I see similarities between what it takes to climb in the mountains and what it takes to rock climb at the edge of one's limit. Both rise from a foundation of desire and work, but then other things start to happen—adversity, chance, immaterial forces. Ultimately, both pursuits are about continued effort in the face of uncertainty, sometimes for days or weeks or months, even years. And you can't flip to the last page to see what happens; you just have to keep going until you get there. Isn't that just like life?

ALL THE WAY: SALATHE FREE

I came home from Patagonia worn into the ground. The trip had started the moment I stepped off the bus in the little Argentine town of El Chalten to find Dean ready to hike straight up into the mountains. The weather had broken clear and windless, almost to the hour upon my arrival. Forty-eight hours of travel had made me a little haggard, but there was no resisting the urgency of perfect weather. I went from Moab to the summit of Standhardt without stopping.

We finished the season exhausted but satisfied. A first ascent on Standhardt, the first one-day ascent of Torre Egger, and a base jump for Dean off El Mocho, a small peak we climbed together. It took us weeks to fully recover from the trip, but I found myself obsessively trying to get back into free climbing fitness as soon as I returned to Moab. I plunged into my standard Moab training regime: lifting weights at the twenty-four-hour Moab fitness center, going for short trail runs, and setting route-length boulder problems on our backyard climbing wall. Dean left for Yosemite in April, but I just wanted to keep training in Moab, with trips to Rifle for steep, pumpy sport climbing.

As April turned to May, Dean got lonely in the Valley, ending every phone call with an increasingly bereft goodbye. I wasn't ready to go to Yosemite yet, but it seemed like I should, being married and all. But I was a little annoyed. Yosemite was flooded, and I didn't see the point of rushing off to California when it was a perfect Moab spring. I decided to head out to Rifle for a last bit of carefree sport climbing, and then just go.

Full of the satisfaction of being a good wife, I packed the car for a two-day trip, rallied Fletcher, and headed out of town. I turned onto the winding River Road from Main Street and immediately got trapped behind a slow-moving SUV with Colorado plates. The classic dilemma—Moab local trying to get somewhere versus meandering tourist with no agenda. There are only a few straight stretches of road, and plenty of dangerous curves above the river, so I got into position for a quick pass by getting right up behind the SUV. I glanced over at Fletch to make sure she was clipped in—a few weeks ago Dean had flown into a panic because Fletcher didn't have a seatbelt—and glanced back to see the SUV in my windshield, brakes on, abruptly turning left into a campground. I drove the brake pedal into the floor, watching in horror as my truck slammed into the back of the SUV. Then I was wedged against an airbag, my forearms burning from the expulsion powder, and my truck was on the shoulder of the wrong side of the road with the horn blaring. The SUV was gone. Dazed, I looked to my right and saw Fletch shaking and panting.

Miraculously, no one was hurt, though both cars were completely totaled and all of us were very shaken up. The SUV had actually flown off the road and landed in a ravine. I never did get the last days in Rifle. Within a week, I had replaced my Ranger with a newer used one from Provo and was driving to Yosemite, Fletcher securely clipped in to her seatbelt. Nothing like a glimpse of death to remind me of the most basic reality. Everything is dangerous. Life is short. I have to make it count.

Yosemite is a hard place for me. Too many people, too many rules. But I also have learned to create some sort of life there. Dean and I bought some land in a privately owned pocket in the Valley and started renting a place to live. For me, having a safe refuge in such a rigidly controlled environment has become necessary.

As I drove west, I thought about the summer and fall to come. I decided I needed a climbing goal to give me the motivation to deal with the aggravating Yosemite lifestyle. I knew that Dean would be completely wrapped up with his own goals and that I would be happier focusing on my own thing, like last season on Free Rider. I pondered the idea of trying to free the Salathe Wall on El Capitan.

It would be a practical project. The Salathe is almost the same route as Free Rider, which I knew quite well. The only difference would be the Salathe headwall pitches. Those pitches are just six hundred feet below the top of El Cap. So, as a solo project, it made all kinds of sense. I could hike up to the top early in the morning, go down to work the headwall pitches until the sun hit them, and be back in the Valley by early afternoon. The predawn morning schedule would suit my natural rhythm perfectly, and I could get a lot of climbing done in the first morning hours of shade while most other routes in Yosemite would be unbearably hot through the summer. There would be no Fletcher-watching dilemmas, even if Dean decided to stay out in the backcountry for days, or kept an unpredictable schedule, since I would be home by early afternoon. And if I managed to decipher those three hard pitches, I could try to rustle up a belayer and go for the route, since I already knew the other thirty-something pitches below. Working the crux of the route would be far more convenient than it had been on Free Rider. I felt a little reluctant because the routes were so similar, though the Salathe headwall seemed so unbelievably hard. I questioned whether it was even a realistic goal. Practicality won out. The Salathe would be inspiring and certainly wouldn't make me any weaker. I arrived in Yosemite with a project.

Fletcher was happier than ever to see all her friends, especially her favorite uncles, Ivo, Chongo, Winky, and Ben. She is more social than I am and seems to really love cruising the Valley with the Yosemite stone monkeys. Though it was early June, the spring wetness was just beginning to dry up. I spent a week correcting the feng shui issues in this season's home base, the downstairs studio of our friends' house in Yosemite West, and once things were auspiciously arranged I began my Salathe mission.

It takes two hours to go up the East Ledges to the top of the Salathe Wall, with good music on the MP3 player and nothing in my pack. My schedule started with waking at 3:00 AM. Trying not to disturb Dean, if he was not already out on some other predawn mission, I would quietly brew espresso, grab some Mojo bars, slip Fletcher a dog biscuit, and head out into the night. During the half-hour drive from Yosemite West I listened to music and eased into consciousness. If I was walking by 4:00, the light would come as I was ascending fixed lines up the side of the East Ledges, and I could turn off my headlamp as I hiked the final slabs over the top of El Cap. By 7:00 AM, I would be on the headwall of the Salathe, warming up alone with a self-belay system on six hundred feet of fixed line. I usually had only a couple tries in me for the long endurance pitch. Then I would stretch out on Long Ledge, cocooned against the morning chill in a light windbreaker, dozing off until I felt strong enough to go back down to piece together the exposed, powerful moves on the second pitch of the headwall, the "boulder problem pitch."

I was not usually nervous alone on El Cap, but the Salathe headwall is an oddly intimidating place. Though I was very used to my solo belay system, having used it to work Free Rider, I felt a little afraid doing dynamic, deadpoint moves where I had to let go of the rock and jump, and for some reason the exposure on the headwall always got to me a little. I worked out a powerful, bouldery sequence for the crux pitch but always had my heart in my throat as I jumped for the first crimps. Good preparation anyway for the lead, I hoped.

After work on the boulder problem pitch, I quickly climbed the bolted "sport pitch" and one more long crack pitch, then got off my belay system and free soloed the 5.6 slab without ropes to the summit. Another hour of work, pulling up ropes and putting things away in the haulbag I was stowing there during the project, and then I was free to run down the East Ledges. I would be back home to a happy Fletch before 3:00 PM, unless Dean or one of the monkeys had already come to rescue her.

The mission was a strenuous workout and usually knocked me out completely for at least two days. Then I would set the alarm and do it again. Despite the soaring temperatures and the inescapable greasiness of the summer granite, I loved having El Cap to myself and having something to keep me busy at a slow summer pace. Gradually the Salathe took hold of me, pulling me into obsession.

Fall arrived, bringing crowds of people and the dreaded Valley crud. I caught the flu but refused to stop, and I ended up too sick to climb for most of September. Suddenly October was upon me.

———————————+———————————

October is a stressful time to be planning a wall route on El Cap. The weather can be perfect and stable, or the first big storm of the season can suddenly bury Yosemite in snow, shutting down any climbing plans for months and even killing people on El Cap. After my summer training days, I was able to consistently climb the endurance pitch without falls on my solo toprope system, and if I gave it my full-on, maximum effort, I could also free the boulder problem pitch. It seemed like it was time to take on the logistics of a free attempt. If I didn't get myself organized quickly, I might miss the opportunity to go for the Salathe this season. I knew that Dean was not interested in spending days on El Cap, belaying and jugging. So I had to find a partner, and I had to figure out how to make that person's life as easy as possible. Mostly, that meant I had to figure out how to eliminate a haulbag on the route.

I stood in the meadow, discussing strategy with my friend Tommy. I wanted to start in the dark and climb to the Alcove, then rest for a day. Then I wanted to climb through the Salathe Roof and go up the fixed lines I had left to Long Ledge. After sleeping and resting there for another day, I would go down to fire the headwall and climb all the way out.

Never one to force his opinions, Tommy offered politely, "Do you want to know what I did the first time I freed the Salathe?"

"Yeah, of course," I answered. I knew Tommy had worked on the route in years past, then had freed it wall-style, and then in a day. I loved hearing the tactics of the top El Cap free climbers—there was a lot to learn from them.

He explained how he had rapped in from above to put a portaledge and haulbag under the Salathe Roof. Then he started the route in the traditional Salathe style, climbing the Free Blast and going down. Then he came back, jugged up and climbed all the way to the portaledge camp, and freed the headwall the next day. He reminded me to keep an open mind about strategy and to do what worked for me.

Until I began living in Yosemite and on El Cap, I hadn't paid much attention to how people climb these hard free routes on El Cap. I had just imagined the climbers to be supernaturally good—they just walked up to the base one day, waltzed up all thirty-something pitches, and then they were done. This perception actually discouraged me from imagining myself trying to do such a big thing. My experience of aid climbing big walls had taught me that they're a lot of work. Nothing goes smoothly or right, nothing is straightforward or normal, and logistics and teamwork are everything.

As I learned about El Cap free climbing firsthand, first from helping Dean prepare for his one-day free linkup of El Cap and Half Dome, and then by absorbing knowledge from the Yosemite climbing community, I realized how uninformed my assumptions had been. And I learned that free climbing El Cap takes a massive amount of preparation and training, sometimes even years' worth, even for the "rock star" climbers. Learning all of this made me see freeing El Cap as a realistic endeavor, rather than an impossible dream.

So they can concentrate on the free climbing, some climbers hire teams of helpers to deal with the problem of moving gear and supplies up and down El Cap. Others recruit their friends to do the things that need doing, like hauling bags up the wall, moving gear to the base or summit, or aiding up pitches to belay the free climbers on toprope so they can work out crux pitches. Some climbers rappel in from above and make stashes for themselves—putting bivy gear, food, and water on the wall—to minimize the grunt work during the ascent. Some climbers come down the wall from above to work out the cruxes on toprope. Some climbers aid up from the bottom, setting topropes on the difficult pitches that are closer to the ground. Many climbers work on their free project for months or even years before they succeed in freeing the entire route.

When it comes time for the ascent, some climbers free pitches in random order, camping at the base of El Cap and going up and down their fixed lines until they have eventually freed all the pitches of the route. Some climbers free the first pitches, rappel to the ground on fixed lines, and jumar up and continue climbing the rest of the route. Some climbers free parts of the route from the ground, then come in from the top to free the upper pitches, while others start up wall-style, then aid out and camp on the top, and then rappel back down to finish the route. Some climbers choose to free the route team-style, with each person only leading half the pitches. Other climbers choose to free as an individual leader, finding a helper to jumar behind them and take care of all the rope work and carry the extra equipment.

As I got clued in to the reality of El Cap free climbing, it appealed to me more and more. People use a mind-blowing array of strategies and methods to pull off their climbs—there is no "official style." Except for one-day climbs, in which the parameters are pretty obvious, almost every free ascent of this huge granite face has used a different approach and style of ascent. This reflects part of what I most love about climbing—the human effort of applying logistics, hard work, and creative thinking to solve nature's challenges.

I thought about the style that mattered most to me in my goal of freeing the Salathe. I liked the concept of leaving the ground and staying up on the wall from then on, even though the traditional way of starting the Salathe is to climb the first twelve to fourteen pitches and then return to the ground, coming back another day to launch onto the wall. When I freed Free Rider in a day, I had already climbed the first thirty pitches of the Salathe in one push, since the two routes share the same start. So I decided I had nothing to prove to myself by eschewing the standard method of starting the Salathe just because I liked the idea of staying up on the wall once I started—it would just be an artificial, token gesture in this case. Climbing the Free Blast and Hollow Flake on a separate climbing day would help with my partner problem, because it would result in one less day that I needed someone to be with me on the wall.

I decided that what was truly important to me was to lead every pitch myself, in order, in a single effort. In Moab, I had freed the Tombstone—a short, multipitch route—with Dean in the team-style method, swinging leads so that we each freed every pitch, but neither of us led every pitch. It was definitely easier to follow the ultralong crux pitch that Dean led, as a toprope is much less demanding than a lead, physically and mentally, especially on a pitch that requires natural gear placements. When a pitch is particularly long, the weight of the lead line is pulling you down, sometimes adding a full grade in difficulty. It was also easier to go for a demanding climb with Dean as my partner. Freeing the route together was a special experience for us as husband and wife, but in my opinion it didn't ask as much from me as a climber. On such a meaningful goal as the Salathe, I wanted the full responsibility of an individual ascent. In my mind, I wouldn't feel that I had really done the route if I didn't lead every crux and manage the entire ascent.

To make this happen, I realized that I needed to place gear stashes on the wall by rappeling in from above with haulbags full of food, water, and camping gear. If my partner had to belay, ascend the rope using jumars, and do all the hauling (as Dean did for me the first time I freed Free Rider), my options would really narrow, because not many people are competent enough to manage such a hard job. If I did the extra work of putting my stashes on the wall, anyone who was strong and fairly competent could come and jumar for me, with very minimal hauling. And I decided to live on the wall, on the natural rock ledges. I liked this idea better than hassling with a portaledge.

My other biggest priority was to climb with the modern free climber's standard, from stance to stance, rather than stopping at old aid hanging belays. Again, my experience with Dean on the Tombstone had been influential in shaping my thoughts about the Salathe. The Tombstone free ascent led me to believe that a long route is not a free climb if you don't climb to natural, hands-off ledges or stances. On multi-pitch routes you often encounter free-hanging belay anchors that past aid parties have drilled into blank sections, which usually turn out to be free climbing cruxes.

The Tombstone had an old aid belay anchor about a hundred feet up the hardest pitch, under a roof, by no means a hands-off stance. Dean felt strongly that the free route had to combine both of the old aid pitches into one massive pitch, from ledge to ledge, or it was still an aid climb—to split the crux pitch into two shorter pitches, with a rest on a hanging belay in the middle, would be much easier to climb but would not be a free ascent. It would be an aid climb with a lot of hard free climbing, or an almost-free climb with a point of aid. Dean saw the Tombstone as not just a first free ascent of a test-piece route but as a physical statement of pure free-climbing standards on multipitch routes.

On the Salathe, I needed to apply this modern free-climbing ethic, climbing past the old anchors on the long endurance pitch of the head-wall to hands-off stances, rather than just clipping the anchors as soon as possible, shouting "Take!" and calling it done, like I would on a sport climb. This was a principle I felt committed to, but it would definitely cause me some headaches!

To carry out my plan, I would need to stash two haulbags on the Salathe's two big ledges, the Alcove and Long Ledge. I would be committed to making it between the stashes, but it would save my partner from doing major hauling on the wall, which would save me a lot of time and energy too. Long Ledge isn't perfectly located, being above the headwall pitches rather than below them. But I could use my fixed line from the summer's training to get to Long Ledge and bivy there for two or three nights while I freed the upper pitches of the Salathe. Though it was only an additional four hundred feet from Long Ledge to the summit, it would be impractical to burn extra energy by jugging out to sleep on top and then rapping back in. I knew I would be more focused and feel more in tune with El Cap if I lived and slept touching the granite. Besides, I liked being on the wall.

Dean assured me there were plenty of monkeys hanging out in the Valley who would love to earn some extra cash by carrying my two haulbags to the top of the Salathe. I needed to start conserving energy and time, and I didn't want to spend the two days it would take me to ferry the bags up there. I packed carefully, buying plenty of food and tasty snacks. I packed an equal amount of vegan food as well as an entire supply of things I don't eat, like tuna, cheese, jerky, bagels, cookies, and candy, for whomever my partner might be. I'd learned that, once on a wall, the vegan food suddenly looks interesting to the nonvegan, sugar-eating climber, so they want everything I eat. But they also need lots more calories and things I would never normally buy. I also scrounged through all of my gear supplies and came up with two sets of sleeping gear for each haulbag as well as two stoves, two espresso makers, and plenty of extras like tape, chalk, socks, and toiletries. Each bag also had five gallons of water. They were fat and full in the back of my truck, but as I trolled around Yosemite Valley, there was an astonishing shortage of available monkeys. The Huber brothers, two of the best and most famous climbers in the world, were doing a film project on El Cap, and they had already cornered the market on dirtbag porters, and at Hollywood prices. I was starting to get stressed out. Finally, I went to the Camp 4 message board and tacked up an ad.

"WANTED: PORTERS. I need two medium haulbags carried to the top of the Salathe, Monday morning. $80 each. Leave a note here. Steph."

Two British guys answered, and I met them the next morning at their campsite. Like Pakistani porters, they were wiry and cheerful. One even had to lash his flapping sneaker sole on with his shoelace, telling me drolly that I could see why he needed the cash. They assured me that the bags weren't too heavy and that they could find the top of the Salathe, although they had never been on the summit of El Cap before. That stressed me out too, but I didn't have any other takers. I left them with the bags, telling the guys that they were full of water and boring vegan food items, and set off up the East Ledges to squeeze in a final workout session on the headwall while they hiked around on the Falls Trail.

Much to my relief, some hours later the Brits popped over the top of El Cap and deposited the heavy bags at the very lip of the Salathe. I spent the next day rapping fifteen hundred feet to the Alcove with the first haulbag hanging between my legs, jugging back to the top for the second one while hauling up my ropes, and then rapping again to Long Ledge to stash the second bag. An unpleasant chore, but finally I stood on the summit knowing I was in perfect position to go for my free attempt. My bags were on the wall, and anyone who could jug competently could be my partner. Finding that person was the final problem, and then I could start thinking about climbing.

I headed down the East Ledges, wondering if I was going to end up with another note on the Camp 4 board: "WANTED: BELAYER. I need someone to jug El Cap and belay for a free attempt on the Salathe. Minimal hauling." I hoped not.

On a steep slab below the Nose I caught up to a wild-looking girl with waist-length blond dreadlocks and a Grade VI haulbag on her back. She told me she had just finished two weeks on the North America Wall. I had found my Salathe partner.

The NA was Cybele's first time up El Cap, but she had done several other aid routes in the Valley. After a five-minute conversation on top of El Cap, Cybele offered to belay me on the Salathe. I always trust my instincts, and there is something I like about just meeting someone and going for a big climb. It can be stressful because the other person's ability and personality are somewhat unknown. It means that I have to feel totally confident in my own ability to get us both up the route, if necessary, and deal with any potential epics. But to me, this style follows the classic Layton Kor climbing tradition and is also a way of embracing uncertainty and the flow of the universe. I often end up with a friend for life. I had a strong feeling that this was how the Salathe should be.

The next day I bumped into Cybele at the post office, and I took it as a sign that I should ask her to go with me on the Salathe. As we talked more, she told me that she had been there when I freed El Cap in a day. She had happened to be walking around the base of El Cap when I started up the first pitch that evening. I had been too focused to notice, but she had talked with Heinz at the base as I began the climb. I didn't need any more messages from the universe. I liked Cybele's energy, and I trusted her. I knew she was the right person.

Cybele had to go back to LA for a few days, so I decided to start the route with Dean, climbing the Free Blast up past the Hollow Flake. I was happy to have him belay me for this involved, up-and-down section of the route, making things run perfectly, and I stashed my rope and rack on the Hollow Flake ledge. Cybele returned from LA, and we jugged up the fixed lines and started the Salathe.

I had planned five days on the wall: three climbing days with two rest days in between. The first day would be hard since we had a lot of vertical gain. It would also be Cybele's and my first climbing day together. I was nervous about the second day, having to climb the Huber Pitch, the dihedrals, and the Salathe Roof. Though I had stuck the Huber Pitch on my one-day climb of Free Rider, after twenty-two pitches of climbing I still dreaded it on this ascent. The sideways jump I have to catch to reach the final handhold is "low percentage," and increased traffic on Free Rider had recently caused one of the setup crimpers to crumble and become less positive. I didn't feel sure I would fire it. I also worried about sending the Salathe Roof after climbing several crux pitches that day. I haven't figured out why it's rated 12a in guidebooks because it seems so difficult. Like the headwall pitches, the hardest moves come at the very end, and I worried about the strenuous, insecure moves over the lip. Cybele would also have to do hauls with our sleeping bags and clothes, which could slow us down. The third climbing day, our fifth day up there, would be the two headwall pitches and the final pitches to the top.

Cybele and I blasted off in the dark, and I started the chimney above Hollow Flake just before dawn. Despite unseasonably hot temperatures that day, the climbing went well, and we spent the next day resting at the Alcove. Cybele turned out to be one of the most interesting people I've ever met, with endless stories and unique world perspectives. Unfortunately the day was not completely relaxing. We heard news of an impending storm. Since the date was exactly one year after the freak October storm that had killed climbers on El Cap, all the weather forecasters were erring on the side of caution, afraid to take a firm position about the storm. We spent the day calling friends on our cell phones, trying to find some consistency in the predictions. I hated to think of going down already, after all of this preparation. We decided to keep going.

We woke in the dark the next day, to start the Huber Pitch in morning shade since it had been so hot the day before. This day dawned stormy and cold instead. I stood at the belay, shivering, and an aid party approached. Rather than waiting at the Sloping Ledge belay below us and giving me a chance to climb this crux, the leader aided right up under me and hung on a piton, waiting. I tried to ignore it and went for the pitch. Nervous and cold, I whipped off the jump move. I lowered back to Cybele, deeply upset. I felt too pressured to rest, so I tried again immediately. This time I got my hand on the big hold but not deep enough to stay on, and I whipped off again. After my third rapid-fire try, nearly in tears and feeling my crimp strength fading on the opening moves, I told the aid climber to just go through. He slowly went up. Instead of backcleaning to leave it clear for me, he left his rope clipped all along the final crack that I would have to reach for after the crux. I waited in disbelief, shaking with cold. Thoughts of rapping filled my mind. Suddenly it started sleeting. I looked at Cybele and started laughing. This scenario seemed like a joke. It could hardly be any more epic. I started up, brushing sleet from the bigger footholds. I stuck the jump, pulled their rope out of my way as I laybacked up the crack, and sped past the other climbers.

I had wasted way too much time and energy on the Huber Pitch. As we reached the Block, it started to rain. We opened the haulbag and crouched inside our bivy sacks, wondering what to do. The rain stopped, winds kicked up, and the rock dried, so I kept climbing up to the strenuous dihedral below the Salathe Roof. Freezing wind blew straight up the giant corner. Miserable and wretched in tight rock shoes and thin clothing, I reached the belay below the roof. Worn out from the cold, I looked up at the daunting roof. I had to climb it now to stay on track for a shot at the headwall. I fought through the Rifle-esque overhangs, trying unsuccessfully to shake the pump out of my rock-hard forearms. Too tired to recover, I rushed into the final crux. My mind blanked. I screwed up my double-knee-scum sequence and gracelessly pawed at the sloping holds over the lip in a last-ditch attempt to hit the final flared handjam. I whipped off, flying into space below the Salathe Roof, thousands of feet off the deck with nothing below me. Believe me when I say that is REALLY scary.

I was too cold and exhausted to try again, but blowing this pitch to-day threw off my plan for the headwall pitches. The day had gone so badly that I knew I should just call this attempt and leave. I felt like I had flailed all day—and I hadn't even reached the headwall yet. But if I bailed now at pitch twenty-eight, there was a chance I wouldn't be able to organize again for another attempt this season. I would have to replace all the wa-ter and food we had used at the Alcove, find another partner, and start all over. It would be more effort to do all that than to keep going, despite how bad things were looking. In terms of effort and supplies, I was fully committed to this seemingly doomed attempt. On the bright side, after this day of repeated falling, I fully trusted Cybele's belay! We got on the fixed lines and went up to Long Ledge to sleep on it.

Fortunately, the storm passed, and we roasted all day in the sun on Long Ledge. El Cap . . . always too hot or too cold. The next morning, we woke up in the dark and rapped back to the roof. With no warm-up, I got instantly flash pumped. My forearms were as hard as rocks, and there was no way to pull the last moves. I lowered down to Cybele, try-ing not to feel demoralized. The Salathe was turning out to be a battle, even more than I had imagined.

On the second try, I finally felt good. I pulled the last moves, this time in control and climbing right, and I heard Dean's characteristic raven call, clear as a bell from El Cap Meadow. I knew that he and Fletcher were down there in the grassy meadow, watching me climb. I wondered when I would see them. I was only three thousand feet away from my little family, but in a whole different world.

It took some time for Cybele to jug and for me to organize the hefty rack for the endurance headwall pitch. As I left the belay, the sun hit the wall, making it hard to see small footholds. I climbed through the lower cruxes and through the increasingly strenuous crack, feeling weak. In the dreaded overhanging flared splitter crack, I climbed until my body couldn't go on, feeling the greasy, sunny rock slime out under my opening hands. It was over.

I didn't know what to do. Things had been going so wrong, ever since the Huber Pitch. I felt like I had struggled all the way up this route, and that maybe I was forcing this attempt when it wasn't meant to be. My last free climb on El Cap had been so magical—not easy, but flowing—and I had wanted to feel like that on the Salathe too, not like I was fighting to the death. But I felt like I hadn't had a real shot at the headwall, which was really the driving force behind climbing all the way up here, on all the same pitches as Free Rider. My original plan was irredeemably shattered. We only had food and water on Long Ledge for two or three days, and we had already spent a rest day on the ledge and this climbing day. I wasn't physically recovered from the trying storm day, despite the rest, and was now even more worked. Realistically, I didn't think I could do the headwall tomorrow. I just wanted one good chance. "So we take another rest day, and you try again," Cybele said reasonably. "We have some food."

We spent another day on Long Ledge, watching the birds and listening to music. The next morning, at first light, we returned to the base of the headwall. I was freezing cold, and my feet were completely numb as I climbed through the lower crux. I kept thinking they would come to life as I warmed up, but even after I fought through the flared splitter, I couldn't feel my toes at all. Giving it everything I had, I tried to place my feet by sight instead of feel on the tiny footholds through the final crux. My right foot popped off as I hit the second-to-last handhold, 150 feet up, and I whipped below the anchor, which I had already clipped. I was two moves away from the hands-off stance above that final anchor. Totally spent, I hung on the rope and felt my feet come back to life. Great.

OPPOSITE: Salathe roof (photo by Jimmy Chin)

Back at Long Ledge, I looked at Cybele shamefacedly. "Cybele, we've been up here seven days. I can't ask you to stay up here any longer. Plus we're almost out of food."

"Hey, at this point, what's another day?" Cybele said. "You fell off the last move. Obviously you can do it. We have a little food. Try again tomorrow."

The next morning, deeply tired, I fell from the flared splitter and finished the pitch with one fall. I had completely underestimated the added difficulty of leading this endurance pitch, having worked it from above, freeing it every time on my toprope system. When I climbed above the pieces at the end of this ultralong pitch, I could feel the weight of the rope pulling me down throughout the most strenuous crux sections. I was leading on the thinnest possible rope, an 8.9 millimeter, but on the last clips of the pitch the cord was so heavy that my thumb couldn't push it into the carabiner gate. I had to get to a stance, pull up a loop of rope, clench it in my teeth, and push the loose section into the biner at waist level. I was so close. But we had been up here for eight days. My muscles weren't recovering. It was starting to look hopeless. Still, the thought of just giving up and forfeiting all the effort didn't feel right.

Demoralized and sad, I told Cybele that I thought we should go down. She'd already been up here longer than I had asked her to be. Plus, she had put her elderly little dog in a kennel in LA to be here and had rented a car to drive out to the Valley. Both were racking up bigger bills by the day. I was torn with guilt, knowing that the geriatric dachshund was all alone in a strange place without her human, all because I selfishly wanted to free the Salathe. But despite a few comments about feeling like she was on Gilligan's Island, Cybele wasn't having any of it.

"Look," she said, "I'm going to jug those fixed lines to the top and go down to the Valley for food. I'll spend the night there and come back the next morning. Then you'll get a rest day and you'll be able to eat tons of food. Your body is getting too weak up here. You hardly eat anything. It seems like you're about to do it. I don't think you should give up just because things haven't been perfect." I was truly awed at Cybele's generosity, and I couldn't believe what she was doing for me. Later she would insist over and over that it was really no big deal. But not many people would be hanging in there with me like this, and I knew my instinct about Cybele had been right on.

I decided that since I had a four-gallon water stash hidden just at the summit, which Cybele would never be able to find, that she shouldn't carry an additional thirty-six pounds of water weight in her pack. I also would certainly never impose on Ivo or Dean or the Valley crew by calling them on my cell phone and ordering them to hike up, get my stash, and rap it in to me as I waited divalike on Long Ledge. Grabbing the water stash would be a ten-minute chore of jugging and rappeling—if that simple task left me too tired to lead the enduro pitch, then it was time to go down anyway!

With Cybele on Long Ledge, Salathe Wall (photo by Jimmy Chin)

When Cybele left, I sat alone on the ledge, missing her company. Hours later, I saw my truck pull away from El Cap Meadow and smiled, watching her drive off in the direction of Yosemite Village.

At this point, it seemed equally likely that I would do this route or that I would fail. I had lost sense of time, but I also felt like I had been on the Salathe forever. As long as it didn't storm and we had food, I actually liked being up here on El Cap. I've spent weeks in a snow cave, and this was pretty luxurious by comparison. What wasn't comfortable was the stress I felt at having put so much into this climb and knowing I probably wouldn't complete it. I also felt sad that things had gone so wrong when I had tried to plan everything perfectly for one good attempt at the Salathe. Partially, my careful plan had slipped out of my control with the other climbers and the storm. But I knew I should have anticipated how much harder the lead would be on the enduro pitch, and maybe I should have tried to lead it a few times last month by rapping in from above. That was my own oversight, and harder to accept. My solo system of working the route had been definitely far less efficient than working it with a partner. I had loved my summer days alone on El Cap, but now I was feeling like I wasn't as ready as I could be to complete this project.

The next morning, Cybele returned triumphantly, bearing spinach, tofu, alfalfa sprouts, salad dressing, nutritional yeast, juice, forks, a full bottle of red wine ("for consolation or victory"), a "You go, girl!" card with a vial of lavender scent labeled "Pussy Power Potion" from my friend Adonia, an astonishing supply of other carefully planned and packed treats, and best of all, a travel Scrabble game. With excitement like this, I could stay up here another week! I felt fortified and ready, but an aid party of four arrived at the headwall. I had learned from the Huber Pitch debacle that when aid climbers approached cruxes of the free route, I was better off just waiting until they climbed through. "What's another day?" had become my new mantra. We played a thrilling game of Scrabble and ate. My harness was starting to feel too big, the leg loops hanging loose. You get what you need, I think, and I figured losing a few pounds could help if I ever got to the boulder problem pitch.

That night I laid in my sleeping bag, looking at the stars. Despite the festivity of new food, psychologically this climb was getting hard. Two extra days in a row on this narrow ledge was a little much. Cybele was a hero, but I couldn't ask her to stay much longer. I couldn't stand the guilt of her elderly dog languishing in the kennel, made worse by the fact that Fletch was comfortably at home with Dean, all because of my climbing project. If I couldn't send the enduro pitch the next day, I was going to call it. At least I would feel like I'd had a real try. At this point, that was all I wanted.

We had a radio that Ivo had given me to take on the wall. The task of perking up my battered spirits was too big for Cybele alone at this point. Our cell phone batteries were on their last legs—from the early days when we were anxiously checking weather reports—and now I lived for the few minutes a day when Ivo's encouraging voice would come onto the radio with his distinctive Bulgarian accent. "Steph. You can do it!! Thomas says you can absolutely send the enduro pitch next try—he fell off the flared part too, and he knows you will get it next time. You are doing super good! We're super impressed that you are not coming down! All the monkeys are rooting for you down here!" He would pass the radio around to a circle of friends in El Cap Meadow, each giving me words of friendship and support. I was in a raw, stripped state, and hearing their voices over the walkie-talkie touched me to tears. It meant so much coming from this tight crew of true, hardcore El Cap climbers, who understood completely why I was still up here.

The next morning, I started up the headwall feeling great, my rack perfect, my feet finally not numb. I got unbelievably pumped through the flared splitter. I fought through the bulging wall to a strenuous stance, so pumped that I couldn't even pull the trigger to place the next cam into the crack, nearly dropping it as I klutzily shoved it against the rock. Finally I got it in and, after another fight, got it clipped. A few more moves, and I was hanging straight-armed off a handjam, trying to recover, staring at the final crux section.

In early September, I had rapped in to work this section and met a climber who had used my rope to play on the headwall. Climbing up that day, I'd realized with horror that my most important foothold in the final crux section had been broken. A crumbly micro-edge, an inch lower than the original smooth, nickel-size edge, was all that remained. Now, instead of climbing hard moves to a useable stance before the last desperate crux, I would have to climb hard moves to no stance into the desperate crux. I immediately went into denial when I realized the foothold was gone. At the time I determined to think positive, take it in stride, and tell myself it didn't really matter since I could still get through the moves. But the truth was that the final crux had become significantly harder without that decent foothold, which was not what I really needed after 140 feet of hard climbing.

"Get mad!" Cybele shouted up, as I stood at the final "rest" stance, shaking out the pump in my arms. The days and the failures up here had taken their toll, and at this point I felt more like a hostage than a warrior. Finally, I embraced the fury that I had been suppressing since the day I discovered that crux foothold was gone. Yes, in fact, I was super pissed that someone had broken it off, just before I was ready to send the Salathe! Exhausted, but full of rage, I climbed ferociously until I was on the last handhold, and I grabbed the flat hand slot like it meant my life this time. I threw my leg up into the hole, with the anchor below my waist, and—hands-free—clipped the rope into it. I started screaming with astonishment. The sun had arrived. As Cybele cleaned gear from the pitch, I decided to leave the boulder problem pitch for tomorrow. At this point, another day didn't matter. Trying the hardest crux pitch in the sun would be silly, and now I really didn't want to blow it.

The next morning I woke feeling like hell, physically and mentally. I was thrilled to have sent the enduro pitch, but the pressure was now huge. After such a long, drawn-out ordeal, it would be heartbreaking not to finish, just fifty feet from freeing this route.

"I feel great," I told Cybele, unconvincingly. I felt horrendous. Sore, worn-out, and kind of sick to my stomach. I swallowed three aspirins and squeezed my shoes on. The crux pitch of the Salathe is not the best warm-up, at 6:00 AM. Unbelievably nervous and tense, I fell again and again on the bouldery, powerful moves of the second headwall pitch, one move higher each time. Cybele tried to calm me, but mentally I was a wreck. I wondered how many times I could stick the first deadpoint moves before my fingers gave out. The sun moved onto the headwall. I tried desperately to empty my mind, but my thoughts spun with how much I had gone through to get here, how much I wanted to go to Patagonia this winter and not be in the grip of a Salathe obsession, how tired and sore my fingers felt. I had focused so hard on the first headwall pitch and now my mind was fried. A little part of me wished I were freeing this route team-style and could have a stress-free toprope up this last crux and just be done. Not very Zen. I was too broken down to even be dismayed at my lack of spirituality.

I started up again, knowing I would try until my fingers gave out. I barely stuck the first deadpoints, my mind full of failure. Just then, a loud whoosh sounded, like a base jumper. Almost in slow motion, in the middle of crux moves, I turned my head. A dark cluster of birds rushed past, the wind from their wings washing over me. Joy rose through my body. The word "MAGIC" flooded my mind, driving everything else out. Immediately, I broke free.

I cranked through the steep finger crack and, with a shout, jumped to the flared handjam at the base of the tiny cave in the middle of the pitch. I crawled in and waited till my breathing slowed. The close air in the little crevice filled with the scent of lavender and sweat, and I waited longer, knowing this was the final test—it was literally now or never. I didn't have it in me to lower all the way back to the anchor again and climb the first part of the pitch if I blew it now. And this last, hardest crux was the one section of the Salathe that I had never consistently been able to climb when I was training.

Emerging from the cave, I stood up aggressively on the tiny footholds and gripped the flat arête above, rocking my body around into the changing corner. I stood up, strenuously balancing into the tight, flaring seam above, and stopped in the precarious position, gathering my force. With detachment, I noticed that I felt nothing. There was nothing to feel. I breathed deeply, brought my feet up to waist level as I clamped onto the slick, rounded layback edges, and floated way out onto the face to catch the final granite knob. I was light as a dandelion seed, completely in control, perfect at last. For a few precious seconds, I reached the inexorable flow I had been craving on the entire route. I was finally free.

--------+--------

For weeks I was in ecstasy. I had given more than I had to the Salathe. I had used every scrap of reserve I possessed and had to fight harder than I ever thought possible to climb it. That, even more than having freed the route, gave me an enormous feeling of confidence, and I was high from elation. For the first time in my life, I truly believed that I could do anything I put my mind to, and it was an amazing feeling.

But after the flush of success faded, I began to feel drained. I have always experienced a matching low after a big climbing high, and this time was no exception. The low was every bit as intense as the high, to a degree I had never experienced before. I was flattened. And for the first time since I'd started climbing, I felt crushed by doubt. On the Salathe, more than any other climb I'd done, I'd succeeded ultimately through sheer refusal to give up. I felt intensely proud of the effort I gave. But from nowhere, I suddenly saw that effort as diametrically opposed to the spiritual philosophies I have been trying so hard to grasp.

I have always revered climbing as a path to knowledge, a way to learn lessons that are lacking in my materialistic, competitive culture. Every Eastern religion I have studied tells the aspirant to surrender to the flow, to never force outcomes. For the first time, I recognized the conflict between my spiritual philosophies and my personal ethic of hard work and determination, and I was filled with confusion. Didn't working on something I couldn't do qualify as "forcing an outcome"? And if I truly practiced the philosophies I aspired to, shouldn't I have given up on the Salathe the first time I ever tried the headwall and found it too hard to do immediately? Every time something went wrong on my free attempt, should I have "surrendered to the flow" and started rappeling instead of refusing to be defeated and persevering with everything I had? And if my goal in life is to become a better person, shouldn't I be teaching myself not to force the outcome? Or would that just be forc-

OPPOSITE: The final crux, Salathe Wall, El Cap (photo by Jimmy Chin)

ing a different outcome? These questions rained down on me, filling me with confusion and angst. I didn't know what to believe anymore.

When you spend a lot of time inside your head, things have to be right in there or nothing else works. For months I struggled through a kind of crisis of faith. Later, in Rifle, a friend would say sensibly, "Obviously you were exhausted after Free Rider and Patagonia and the Salathe. That's what happens—your adrenal system was shot." Whatever the cause, hollowness consumed me, physically and spiritually. For the first time since I'd started climbing, I questioned my motivation. I felt fragile and helpless in the face of my emotions, and I insulated myself from people even more than usual. I didn't have the strength to stay centered in my own mind, and I had become too sensitive to handle the force of outside energy.

I have to admit, when I first started climbing I assumed I was on a path and that eventually I would get "there." I loved that feeling. Now I am starting to discover that there is no "there," and there may not even be a path most of the time. I hear a lot of voices and a lot of ideas swirling around. It can be hard to figure out what I really think about anything. In some ways it seems like the answer is buried inside the question, and maybe I'll never be able to pull them apart. Maybe I shouldn't even try. In a way, I wish for the clarity I once believed in, though perhaps it was naive. I think some things, the good things, really are that simple . . . Fletch, touching rock, living naturally, breathing, moving, laughing.

In the last few months, surrounding myself with true friends and their positive energy, I am unfolding, emerging renewed. Climbing, I touch rock and feel the rush of infatuation. In a way, it feels like being reborn. I will always push hard. At times, I will be caught by inspiration, and when that happens I will never give up. That's who I am. But what I know now is that climbing is more than that. I'm more than that. So much has happened, but in some ways nothing has changed. Climbing, simply and joyfully, is the way I love the world.

ACKNOWLEDGMENTS

Grateful acknowledgement goes to Kate Rogers, Christine Hosler, and Cassandra Conyers from The Mountaineers Books for their guidance, editing, and patience. Also, thanks to the following excellent editors who helped instigate and improve many of the stories in this book: Nora Gallagher, Jim Little, John Dutton, Jeff Achey, Christian Beckwith, Duane Raleigh, and Steve Roper.

Much appreciation to these superb photographers for their generous contribution: Jimmy Chin, Heinz Zak, Eric Perlman, Kennan Harvey, Charlie Fowler, and Dean Potter.

To these wonderful people, for encouragement and support far beyond the realm of "business," my heartfelt gratitude: Jeanne O'Brien, Karen t'Kint, Jane Sievert, Mark Galbraith, Dylan Seguin, and Craig Holloway.

Truest thanks to all my trusted friends for help, comfort, and wisdom at key moments, especially Lisa Hathaway, Brad Lynch, Jimmy Chin, Ivo Ninov, Adonia Curry Ripple, Laurie Stowe, Virgil Davis III, Dean Fidelman, Karen Roseme, Ron Kauk, and Rick and Annie Cashner.

Thanks most of all to my parents, Virgil and Connie Davis, and, of course, to Fletchmama, without whom there wouldn't be any stories.

PHOTO CREDITS AND REPRINT PERMISSIONS

Jimmy Chin photographs appear on pages 8, 56, 97, 120, 160, 176, 179, and 185.

Steph Davis photographs appear on pages 16, 68, 70, 77, 80, 82, 84, 91, 95, 99, 101, 115, 135, 138, 141, 144, 149, and 158.

Photographs from the Steph Davis collection appear on pages 22, 64, and 144.

Charlie Fowler photographs appear on pages 28 and 34.

Kennan Harvey photographs appear on pages 27, 38, 45, 73, and 104.

Eric Perlman photographs appear on page 109 and on the front cover.

Dean Potter photographs appear on pages 12, 132, 151, and 153.

Heinz Zak photographs appear on pages 32, 112, 121, 125, and 130, and on the back cover.

Quotations from Rumi on pages 5, 9, 57, 85, 105, and 133: Reproduced by permission from Coleman Barks, *The Essential Rumi* (San Francisco, CA: HarperSanFrancisco, 1995).

Quotations from B. K. S. Iyengar on pages 17, 39, 113, and 161. Reproduced by permission of HarperCollins UK from B. K. S. Iyengar, *Light on Yoga* (New York, NY: Schocken Books, 1979).

"Falling" first appeared in *The Mountain Yodel* 7 (1998): 10.

"The Rock & I" first appeared as a "Field Report" in the "Early Spring" Patagonia catalog, 2000.

"Maybe the Swiss Were Right" first appeared in *Rock & Ice* 95 (October 1999).

"A Crack in the Window" first appeared as a "Field Report" in Patagonia's "Alpine Newsletter," October 1997.

"In the Land of Kyrgyzstan" first appeared as "Pictures from Kyrgyzstan" in *Ascent* 14, (1999).

"On My Own" first appeared as "Holding Her Own: Solo in the Ak-Su" in *Rock & Ice* 83 (January 1998): 74–76.

"Four Thousand Pull-Ups" first appeared as "Power of Friendship," MountainZone.com, August 2000, *http://climb.mountainzone.com/2000/elcap/html*.

"Out of Bounds" first appeared in *Climbing* 208 (December 15, 2001): 74–81, 136–7.

"House of Wind" first appeared in Patagonia's "Mountain Book," 2000.

"We've Always Run" first appeared in the Spring 2002 Patagonia catalog.

"Traveling Light" first appeared in the Summer 2004 Patagonia catalog.

"Eternal Sunrise" first appeared in the Spring 2003 Patagonia catalog.

"About Time" first appeared as part of "A Season in Patagonia" on MountainZone.com, February 22, 2001, http://climb.mountainzone.com/2001/patagonia/html/update-022301-sd.html.

"Breaking Free" first appeared in *Climbing* 234 (October 2004): 61–67, 105.

ABOUT THE AUTHOR

Steph Davis is a professional climber and base jumper living in Moab, Utah. She has been featured in *Outside*, *Men's Journal*, *W Magazine*, *National Geographic Adventure*, and *Sports Illustrated*. Her own writing has appeared in *Climbing*, *Ascent*, and *Rock & Ice*, among other publications. Visit her website and blog at highinfatuation.com.

THE MOUNTAINEERS, founded in 1906, is a nonprofit outdoor activity and conservation club, whose mission is "to explore, study, preserve, and enjoy the natural beauty of the outdoors. . . ." Based in Seattle, Washington, the club is now one of the largest such organizations in the United States, with seven branches throughout Washington State.

The Mountaineers sponsors both classes and year-round outdoor activities in the Pacific Northwest, which include hiking, mountain climbing, ski-touring, snow-shoeing, bicycling, camping, kayaking and canoeing, nature study, sailing, and adventure travel. The club's conservation division supports environmental causes through educational activities, sponsoring legislation, and presenting informational programs. All club activities are led by skilled, experienced volunteers, who are dedicated to promoting safe and responsible enjoyment and preservation of the outdoors.

If you would like to participate in these organized outdoor activities or the club's programs, consider a membership in The Mountaineers. For information and an application, write or call The Mountaineers, 7700 Sand Point Way NE, Seattle, Washington 98115; 206-521-6001.

The Mountaineers Books, an active, nonprofit publishing program of the club, produces guidebooks, instructional texts, historical works, natural history guides, and works on environmental conservation. All books produced by The Mountaineers fulfill the club's mission.

Send or call for our catalog of more than 500 outdoor titles:

The Mountaineers Books
1001 SW Klickitat Way, Suite 201
Seattle, WA 98134
800-553-4453
mbooks@mountaineersbooks.org
www.mountaineersbooks.org

OTHER TITLES YOU MIGHT ENJOY BY
THE MOUNTAINEERS BOOKS

The Art of Rough Travel: From the Peculiar to the Practical, Advice from a 19th-Century Explorer
Sir Francis Galton, Edited by Kitty Harmon
Both deliciously bizarre and surprisingly relevant for 21st-century adventurers!

**Rock Climbing:
Mastering Basic Skills**
Craig Luebben
A Mountaineers Outdoor Expert
title for new or intermediate climbers.

**Don't Forget the Duct Tape:
Tips & Tricks for Repairing &
Maintaining Outdoor & Travel Gear,
2nd Edition**
Kristin Hostetter
A must-have for every adventurer!

**A Blistered Kind of Love:
One Couple's Trial by Trail**
Angela and Duffy Ballard
Hilarious, touching account of a couple's
2,650-mile walk in the woods.

**Miles From Nowhere:
A Round-the-World Bicycle Adventure**
Barbara Savage
Funny, honest, poignant account of a
two-year journey. More than 60,000 copies sold!